Legal Forms, Contracts, and Advice for Horse Owners

Legal Forms, Contracts, and Advice for Horse Owners

Sue Ellen Marder, LLM

For information address:
Breakthrough Publications, Inc.
Ossining, New York 10562

ISBN: 0-914327-37-2

Library of Congress Catalog Card Number: 90-85518

Printed in Mexico

99 98 97 96 95 94   5 4 3

Contents

Introduction

This book aims to inform people how they may protect themselves in horse-related business contracts. Too often horse transactions are conducted verbally and the final agreement is never written down. Each person may walk away from the deal with a different translation of what was said. Even more frequently, the parties involved may not anticipate the consequences of the arrangement or unforeseen situations that may intervene. Those who have had any experience with horses know that the old axiom, "what can go wrong does go wrong," was never truer. This book may ease the horse owner through those problems, avoiding lawsuits, financial loss, and hurt feelings.

Horses have become big business in this country. Breeding, raising, racing, showing, and selling horses require a tremendous capital outlay and are subject to many financial and personal considerations. I cannot cover here the many intricacies individual situations may present. Some of the transactions discussed are complicated, and the advice of an attorney should *always* be sought to ascertain the long-range effects as well as the short-term benefits of planning decisions. This book, however, should make horse owners or investors more aware of their options and suggest areas of complexity that require documentation to reduce their potential liability.

I include in each chapter sample forms that illustrate the most general and frequent uses of the basic legal contract. At the end of the book, in an appendix, is a selection of blank forms of the more routine legal contracts. But these forms are supplied merely as guides and are not meant to replace legal counsel.

In Chapter 1 is a discussion of the different ways of forming a horse business and a description of the advantages and disadvantages of the sole proprietorship; the limited and general partnerships; the corporation and the S corporation; and syndications. Individual case studies are included with legal forms for illustrative purposes where applicable. In the chapters which follow, the sample contracts are relevant whether the individual is operating as a sole proprietor or within a partnership or a corporation. Often there are unique personal considerations that alter the standard contract. Blank forms are not supplied at the back of the book when the complexity of the agreement would require legal assistance.

Apart from the first chapter, each chapter is introduced by a description of a typical situation that might face a rider, horse owner, or investor. A sample legal form is proposed and completed, based on the needs of the person(s) in the example. The form is followed by a careful point-by-point discussion of the terms in the contract.

The six questions most often asked regarding legal forms follow. I give a direct and immediate answer to each, but, in fact, this entire book is devoted to answering questions such as these.

Q. *At what point is an "agreement" a legally binding contract?*

A. You are in a legally binding contract at the point you commit the agreement to a signed writing and some form of payment, called "consideration," has passed between the parties. This consideration, usually money, may be a small token of the entire transaction. No minimum percent is required.

Q. *Is it possible to create a contract without having it in writing?*

A. Yes, if certain factors are present. You have a contract if one person has made promises and the second person has relied on those promises to his detriment (suffered some kind of damage or given up something). In this event, the first person is now obligated as if a written contract had been signed. This is where disputes can arise, because each person's memory of a conversation may be different. Reminder: Get everything in writing.

Q. *Does it matter who writes the contract?*

A. Yes. Always draft your own contract. You may write it yourself (with the help of this book) or hire a lawyer to write it. This may seem like more work or expense at the time, but the party that writes the agreement has a definite advantage. The writer provides the clauses he wants included as well as the most beneficial wording. The other party has the opportunity to request changes but often the document retains the flavor (or bias) of the drafter. I am *not* implying any underhandedness here, but simply suggesting procedures that protect a person's self-interest.

In addition, if both parties draft contracts, these can form the basis of negotiation and compromise. In other words, knowing where you both start, you can work toward a middle ground.

Too often, a person signs a paper without fully reading it or understanding its impact. That won't happen to you if you or your representative wrote it.

Q. *Is there any special wording required in an agreement?*

A. No, yet the more precise the language, the more likely it will not be misinterpreted or create issues that might be disputed at a later date.

Q. *What is the most common weakness of many contracts?*

A. They are overly simplistic. Neither side anticipates the possible contingencies in the event the business transaction does not go as planned. Consult a professional in the horse business to clarify the possible problems that may arise so that all angles are covered within the document. This saves legal fees and irritation later.

Q. *What are the basic elements of a written agreement?*

A. The following is a checklist of items to be considered when preparing an agreement. Terms can be added or deleted, depending upon the nature of the contract:
- Names and full addresses of all parties
- Description of the horse(s) if applicable
- Purpose of agreement

- Date of delivery, or point at which contract begins
- Duration of agreement
- Financial terms of agreement
- Payment of additional expenses
- Care of the horse
- Risk of loss if the horse dies or if someone is hurt
- Arbitration of disputes
- Indemnification (who is entitled to reimbursement if someone is sued)
- Termination of agreement: grounds, notice
- Date of agreement
- Signatures

Each of these terms will be discussed in more detail within the following chapters.

1

Different Ways of Doing Business

Choosing the best method (and contract) for operating a horse business is a complex decision. Sometimes the business evolves naturally, based on the owner's needs and priorities, but usually this area requires good professional counseling because every business and business contract has legal consequences. The Tax Reform Act of 1986 and its subsequent revisions have further complicated this area. (See companion book, L. A. Winter and S. E. Marder, *Tax Planning and Preparation for Horse Owners*, Breakthrough Publications, 1991.)

In general, start the simplest type of business and use the simplest contract possible under the circumstances. The catch is obvious: circumstances may dictate a more complex business form than would be normally required. Many different business arrangements can be made, but we are now going to examine several of the most common, including sole proprietorships, partnerships, and corporations.

SOLE PROPRIETORSHIP

The simplest type of business is the sole proprietorship. The person with the knowledge and skill manages the business alone and puts in his or her own money.

> **Example.** Nancy B. wants to open a riding stable. She has saved $10,000, to cover start-up costs. She already owns a few school horses and has converted the family farm into a six-stall barn with several paddocks and a ring. As an experienced show rider, she plans to instruct riders and use a few youngsters to help her part-time with stable chores.

The sole proprietorship is a practical way of doing business for Nancy. She has the necessary expertise to run the business herself and wants to keep the business small. Her funds are limited, but enough to cover start-up costs. At this point, she doesn't want the additional expense of incorporation. She will file her personal tax return with Schedule F, since she is running a farm and is self-employed.

She also takes out an insurance policy with a $2,000 premium, covering her personal liability up to $150,000 per accident in case someone is injured on the property. In addition, she plans to require that a release form be signed by each parent and rider. These forms state that the person who signs recognizes the risks inherent in all horse-related activities and will not sue the owner of the farm or the instructor for any injuries connected with the riding program. (See Chapter 11, "Release and Hold Harmless Agreements.")

PARTNERSHIP

A partnership exists under the Tax Code when two or more people carry on any form of business with each person contributing money, property, labor or skill, and all members expecting to share in the profits and losses (Code Sec. 761).

> **Example.** Silas and Jenny, both experienced stable managers and riders, decide to leave their lucrative jobs and live in poverty by buying and selling show horses. They plan to pool their savings and share all responsibilities of this new venture. Silas and Jenny are in business together. They are contributing money, labor, and skill, and both plan to share profits and losses. By definition, they are not sole proprietors, but are partners.

The partnership form of operating a horse business has become increasingly popular with the rising price of horses and the costs of racing, breeding, or showing. It provides the means to spread expenses and risks, but with its growing use have come increasingly complex tax rules affecting partnerships.

Although a partnership is not taxed as such, its taxable income for the year must be computed and an information return must be filed reporting the partnership income, expenses, gains, and losses. This taxable income is then divided among the partners and reported by each partner on his individual return.

Election Not to Be Taxed As a Partnership

Under certain circumstances, all members of a partnership may elect not to be treated as partners, i.e., to file returns as individuals without the partnership information form. To make such an election, the partnership must be formed solely for investment purposes or for the purpose of using property without selling services or selling the property produced. Most horse businesses do not fit within these exceptions.

Sometimes a stallion breeding partnership is formed for servicing the mares of partners. In this case, a statement would be attached to the partnership information tax return for the first year. After that, the partners would file as individuals without the partnership return.

Material Participation Rules

As a partner or sole proprietor, the investor in the horse business must face passive loss limitations. If the person is not actively involved in the horse business, the losses from this activity will not be allowed to offset other income from a salary, business, or investment portfolio (for instance, dividends).

Generally, all work done in connection with the business, from mucking stalls to attending horse shows to evaluating a horse's performance, counts toward hours spent. Horses don't respect office hours, so the twelve- to sixteen-hour day is unfortunately not uncommmon. The surest way to qualify is to participate in the activity for more than 500 hours during the year, but an individual can also qualify with more than 100 hours during the year as long as he or she participates on a regular, continuous, and substantive basis.

Nancy B., the sole proprietor, as well as Silas and Jenny, the partners, easily qualify as active participants in their businesses. The care and management of horses is labor intensive.

On the other hand, an investor who provides money but hires others to run the business will probably fail the test for active participation. If the taxpayer does not put in the requisite hours, he or she will not be able to deduct horse business losses from other income such as salary or dividends and interest. (See *Tax Planning and Preparation for Horse Owners.*)

The following form is the partnership agreement entered into by Silas and Jenny. Theirs is a very basic agreement stating their purpose to buy and sell horses, along with an allocation of their financial interests.

SAMPLE

PARTNERSHIP AGREEMENT

THE PARTNERSHIP AGREEMENT is made this _____ day of _____, 19_____, by and between ___Jenny W._____ and ___Silas M._____ .

EXPLANATORY STATEMENT

The parties hereto desire to enter into the business of ____purchasing, acquiring, owning and selling horses and ponies and engaging in any other lawful phase or aspect of the horse business._____ .
In order to accomplish their aforesaid desires, the parties hereto desire to join together in a general partnership under and pursuant to any applicable state code.

NOW, THEREFORE, in consideration of their mutual promises, covenants, and agreements, and the Explanatory Statement, which is incorporated by reference herein and made a substantive part of this Partnership Agreement, the parties hereto do hereby promise, covenant and agree as follows:

Section 1. Name.

The name of the partnership shall be _____ ''Centaur Associates'' .

Section 2. Principal Place of Business.

The principal place of business of the Partnership (the ''Office'') shall be located at

_____

_____

_____

Section 3. Business and Purpose.

3.1 The business and purposes of the Partnership are to __acquire, hold, manage, sell and lease horses and ponies (the ''Property''), or interests therein, and to engage in any other phase or aspect of the horse business_____ .

3.2 The Partnership may also do and engage in any and all other things and activities and have all powers incident to the said acquisition, holding, management, sale and leasing of the Property, or any part or parts thereof.

Section 4. Term.

The Partnership shall commence upon the date of this Agreement, as set forth above and shall terminate pursuant to the further provisions of this Agreement.

Section 5. Capital Contributions.

5.1 The original capital contributions to the Partnership of each of the Partners shall be made concurrently with their respective execution of this Agreement in the following dollar amounts set forth after their respective names:

Jenny W.	$_____
Silas M.	$_____

5.2 An individual capital account shall be maintained for each Partner. The capital account of each Partner shall consist of his or her original capital contribution, increased by (a) additional capital contributions made by him or her, and (b) his or her share of Partnership profits, and decreased by (i) distributions of such profits and capital to him or her, and (ii) his or her share of Partnership losses.

5.3 Except as specifically provided in this Agreement, or as otherwise provided by and in accordance with law to the extent such law is not inconsistent with this Agreement, no Partner shall have the right to withdraw or reduce his or her contributions to the capital of the Partnership.

Section 6. Profit and Loss.

6.1 The percentages of Partnership Rights and Partnership Interest of each of the Partners in the Partnership shall be as follows:

Jenny W.	50%
Silas M.	50%

6.2 For purposes of Sections 702 and 704 of the Internal Revenue Code of 1986, or the corresponding provisions of any future federal Internal Revenue law, or any similar tax law of any state or jurisdiction, the determination of each Partner's distributive share of all items of income, gain, loss, deduction, credit or allowance of the Partnership for any period or year shall be made in accordance with, and in proportion to, such Partner's percentage of Partnership Interest as it may then exist.

Section 7. Distribution of Profits.

The net cash from operations of the Partnership shall be distributed at such times as may be determined by the Partners in accordance with Section 8 of this Agreement among the Partners in proportion to their respective percentages of Partnership Interest.

Section 8. Management of the Partnership Business.

8.1 All decisions respecting the management, operation and control of the Partnership business and determinations made in accordance with the provisions of this Agreement shall be made only by the unanimous vote or consent of all of the Partners.

8.2 The Partners shall devote to the conduct of the Partnership business as much of their respective time as may be reasonably necessary for the efficient operation of the Partnership business.

Section 9. Salaries.

Unless otherwise agreed by the Partners in accordance with Section 8 of this Agreement, no partner shall receive any salary for services rendered to or for the Partnership.

Section 10. Legal Title to Partnership Property.

Legal title to the property of the Partnership shall be held in the name of ____Centaur Associates_____. or in such other name or manner as the Partners shall determine to be in the best interest of the Partnership.

Section 11. Banking.

All revenue of the Partnership shall be deposited regularly in the Partnership savings and checking accounts at such bank or banks as shall be selected by the Partners.

Section 12. Books; Fiscal Year;

Accurate and complete books of account shall be kept by the Partners and entries promptly made therein of all of the transactions of the Partnership, and such books of account shall be open at all times to the inspection and examination of the Partners.

Section 13. Transfer of Partnership Interest and Partnership Rights.

Except as otherwise provided in Sections 14, 15 and 16 hereof, no Partner (hereinafter referred to as the ''Offering Partner'') shall, during the term of the Partnership, sell, hypothecate, pledge, assign or otherwise transfer with or without consideration (hereinafter collectively referred to as a ''Transfer'') any part or all of his Partnership Interest or Partnership Rights in the Partnership to any other person (a ''Transferee''), without first offering (hereinafter referred to as the ''Offer'') that portion of his Partnership Interest and Partnership Rights in the Partnership subject to the contemplated transfer (hereinafter referred to as the ''Offered Interest'') first to the Partnership, and, secondly, to the other Partners, at a purchase price (hereinafter referred to as the ''Transfer Purchase Price'') and in a manner as agreed.

Section 14. Purchase Upon Death.

14.1 Upon the death of any Partner (hereinafter referred to as the ''Decedent'') the Partnership shall neither be terminated nor wound up, but instead, the business of the Partnership shall be continued as if such death had not occurred. Each Partner shall have the right of testamentary disposition to bequeath all or any portion of his Partnership Interest and Partnership Rights in the Partnership to a member of his immediate family or to any trust in which any one or more members of the immediate family retain the full beneficial interests.

14.2 The aggregate dollar amount of the Decedent Purchase Price shall be payable in cash on the closing date, unless the Partnership shall elect prior to or on the closing date to purchase the Decedent Interest in installments as provided in Section 19 hereof.

Section 15. Purchase Upon Bankruptcy or Retirement.

15.1 Upon the Bankruptcy or Retirement from the Partnership of any Partner (the ''Withdrawing Partner''), the Partnership shall neither be terminated nor wound-up, but, instead, the business of the Partnership shall be continued as if such Bankruptcy or Retirement, as the case may be, had not occurred, and the Partnership shall purchase and the Withdrawing Partner shall sell all of the Partnership Interest and Partnership Rights (the "Withdrawing Partner's Interest") owned by the Withdrawing Partner in the Partnership on the date of such Bankruptcy or retirement (the "Withdrawal Date").

Section 16. The Appraised Value.

The term "Appraised Value", as used in this Agreement, shall be the dollar amount equal to the product obtained by multiplying (a) the percentage of Partnership Interest and Partnership Rights owned by a Partner by (b) the Fair Market Value of the Partnership's assets.

Section 17. Notices.

Any and all notices, offers, acceptances, requests, certifications and consents provided for in this Agreement shall be in writing and shall be given and be deemed to have been given when personally delivered against a signed receipt or mailed by registered or certified mail, return receipt requested, to the last address which the addressee has given to the Partnership.

Section 18. Governing Law.

It is the intent of the parties hereto that all questions with respect to the construction of this Agreement and the rights, duties, obligations and liabilities of the parties shall be determined in accordance with the applicable provisions of the laws of the State of ___Maryland___.

Section 19. Miscellaneous Provisions.

19.1 This Agreement shall be binding upon, and inure to the benefit of, all parties hereto, their personal and legal representatives, guardians, successors, and their assigns to the extent, but only to the extent, that assignment is provided for in accordance with, and permitted by, the provisions of this Agreement.

19.2 Nothing herein contained shall be construed to limit in any manner the parties, or their respective agents, servants, and employees, in carrying on their own respective business or activities.

19.3 The Partners agree that they and each of them will take whatever actions as are deemed by counsel to the Partnership to be reasonably necessary or desirable from time to time to effectuate the provisions or intent of this Agreement.

19.4 This Agreement and exhibits attached hereto set forth all (and are intended by all parties hereto to be an integration of all) of the promises, agreements, conditions, understandings, warranties and representations among the parties hereto with respect to the Partnership, the business of the Partnership and the property of the Partnership, and there are no promises, agreements, conditions, understandings, warranties or representations, oral or written, express or implied, among them other than as set forth herein.

IN WITNESS WHEREOF, the parties have hereunto set their hands and seals and acknowledged this Agreement as of the date first above written.

WITNESS:

_____
Jenny W.

Percentage of Partnership Interest and Partnership Rights

_____ (SEAL) _____%

Residence Address: _____

_____

_____

Silas M.

_____ (SEAL) _____%

Residence Address: _____

_____

IN WITNESS WHEREOF, I have hereunto set my hand and seal as of the date first above written.

WITNESS: _____

_____ (SEAL)

Discussion of Sample Partnership Agreement

This general partnership agreement may seem complicated, but in fact, it has been simplified. Most fledgling partnerships will require professional counsel because there are several complex issues to resolve.

The agreement begins with the date and the names of the partners.

The Explanatory Statement describes the purpose of the agreement in general terms. The relevant body of state law is also alluded to here. The following sections are the basic elements of the agreement:

1. The name of the partnership is stated.

2. The place of business is given with a full address.

3. The general purpose of the business is stated, in this case to sell and lease horses and ponies. The powers necessary to engage in this business are given to the partners.

4. The term of the agreement can be set here. In this example, the date of termination is indefinite.

5. This section clarifies the financial commitments by listing the capital contributions. In addition, the system of accounting for each partner's interest is described.

6. The percentages of each partner's interest is designated as 50%. Each partner will receive his or her profits and losses based on this percent.

7. The profits will be distributed at times designated by the partners. At this point in most partnership agreements, there would be a detailed definition of net cash and taxable income for federal income tax purposes.

8. All agreements made by the partnership require a unanimous vote or consent of both members.

They both agree to devote as much time to the business as necessary.

9. No partner receives a salary. They receive distributions of profits instead.

10. All legal title of partnership property is held in the name of the partnership unless they agree otherwise.

11. The partnership maintains a separate bank account.

12. The books must be kept accurately and are open to each partner's inspection.

13. One partner cannot transfer his interest without first giving the other partner the option to buy him out. The transfer purchase price based on the appraised value can be a very complex section including the determination of appraised value and the rules for selling an interest.

14. The transfer of the interest on death can be highly complex, stating the procedures for heirs to notify other partners and the procedure for purchasing the decedent's interest. The partnership can be terminated in the event of a death.

15. The purchase upon bankruptcy or retirement is another option which requires one partner to sell his interest to the other partner(s). The procedure for this sale can be set out in full detail.

16. The appraised value is explained in a deceivingly simple formula, but this is a very complex calculation better left to professionals.

17. All notices must be in writing personally delivered or sent by certified mail.

18. The state of governing law is named.

19. Under miscellaneous provisions, this agreement shall be binding on any person who receives a partnership interest through one of the existing partners.

Nothing in the agreement should control how the individual partners run another business.

This agreement is intended as an integration of all verbal statements and stands as the sole agreement.

Some agreements include requirements that each partner has a will authorizing the execution of the partnership interest as stated in the agreement.

Finally, the agreement is signed by each partner and the percent of his partnership interest and his address is noted. It is witnessed by another person.

This general partnership agreement is meant as a sample to help the reader better understand the general nature and scope of the form.

LIMITED PARTNERSHIP

A limited partnership is one in which one or more partners have limited liability. Limited liability means a partner's losses cannot exceed a predetermined amount. If the business were to be sued, the partner would not bear the cost beyond this set figure. In addition, a limited partnership must have one or more general partners who do not have limited liability and who normally manage the partnership.

> **Example:** Marielle has the expertise to run a riding business. Several of her wealthy friends would like her to open her own stable. They take lessons from her, but they do not have the time or experience to help her run the business. Marielle suggests that three of her clients form a limited partnership of which she will be general partner and will work full-time to manage the business. The investors will provide the working capital and will own an interest in the business. The responsibilities and obligations of the respective parties are to be set out in a limited partnership agreement.

A limited partnership agreement requires a list of the rights and powers of the general partner, Marielle, versus the rights and powers of the limited partners, her friends. The accounting system is much more complex because the entire agreement is a meshing of two groups with different liabilities and financial commitments to the partnership.

Furthermore, the income or losses allocated to the limited partners are, by law, passive income. Horse owners and breeders are aware of a provision in the tax code that limits the deduction of losses from any business activity in which a person does not "materially participate," i.e., passive losses. Consequently, fewer people may be willing to invest in the highly risky business of horses without tax incentives; thus, the limited partnership is not as favorable an option as it was in the past.

A sample of a limited partnership agreement is not included here because persons contemplating limited partnerships should seek professional guidance.

SYNDICATIONS

Syndication is a relatively familiar term in the horse world, but the word is somewhat misleading. Under the tax law, a syndicate is not a separate way of doing business. Depending upon the particular arrangement and its activities, a syndicate created to breed, race, or show horses may be either a partnership or a joint ownership.

Although it is more desirable to treat a syndicate as a co-ownership of property, this is not always possible. Under the tax law, a partnership exists when two or more persons join together to carry on a business and share in the profits and losses. A partnership return is required, which adds time, expense, and complexity. The examples which follow will show the difference between two types of syndications.

Syndicate As Co-ownership

- Stallion syndicate in which breeding rights are reserved to the shareholders and NO breeding services are sold to the public by the syndicate.
- Joint ownership of a show horse as an investment.

Syndicate As Partnership

- Syndicate owns a stallion and sells breeding rights to non-syndicate members.
- Syndicate owns the broodmare(s) and sells the foals.
- Syndicate owns the race horse(s) and shares in the purses.

In all forms of syndication, the investors share the expense, and reduce their risks by allowing each investor to buy a share in one or more horses, or by ensuring breeding rights in a particular stallion. It is a form of group ownership, usually formed for a particular short-term purpose.

Because of the recent tax changes and because syndication agreements vary greatly, each carrying different tax benefits and liabilities, the investor must seek professional advice. Also, in addition to tax impact, investors may be subject to state and federal securities laws.

When a person is relatively uninformed and unskilled and then turns over his money to others relying on their professional or management skill to manage it, the transaction is called an investment security. Under federal law, selling unregistered securities is a criminal act, punishable by a fine of up to $10,000 or imprisonment for five years, or both. Preparing and filing a registration statement is a lengthy and expensive procedure, although where the offering is made to a limited number of people or involves relatively small amounts of money, there are exceptions to the registration requirement. The person selling interests, as well as the investor, must seek legal counsel before creating a limited partnership or other organization in which interests will be sold.

Example: Two friends wish to buy a show horse of Olympic potential. One can't afford the cost of buying the horse alone. The second friend is not a serious rider but loves the thrill of seeing the horse they own in the show ring. They need a syndicate agreement that is a co-ownership. It sets forth the rights and obligations of each of them under a syndication agreement. Syndication agreements can run 150 pages alone, but the one that follows, with only two persons involved, has been kept very simple.

SAMPLE

SYNDICATE

AGREEMENT, made _____April, 1990_____ between the persons whose names and addresses are set out in the Schedule attached and who have subscribed for the number of units set forth opposite their names ("Owners").

RECITALS

The Owners desire to form a Syndicate to purchase the __gelding Hope and Glory, quarterhorse, foaled 1980__ herein referred to as the "horse".

The Owners will pay the sum of $ __6,250.00__ per unit. There shall be __10__ units in this Syndicate. __Nancy Rider__, acting for this Syndicate shall purchase the horse for the sum of $ __62,500.00__ and will accept delivery of the horse.

Upon said purchase of the horse, the Syndicate shall be in existence for the ownership and management of the horse upon the following terms and conditions:

1. Ownership.

The ownership of the horse shall be __10__ units, to be insured at a price of $ __6,250.00__ per unit; each of the __10__ units be on an equal basis with the others, and only a full unit shall have any rights.

2. Location.

The horse shall be stabled at __Springs Farm on Fireplace Road, East__, __Hampton, New York 11937__ subject to change by consensus, and shall be under the personal supervision of __Nancy Rider__, as Syndicate Manager.

3. Manager's Duties.

Subject to the approval of the Partner(s), the Syndicate Manager shall have full charge of and control over the management of the horse and of all training matters arising out of this enterprise, subject to the approval of the Owners.

She shall keep accurate account of all show records. She shall exercise her best judgment in all training decisions.

4. Transferability.

Units may be transferred subject to the terms of this agreement; provided, however, that each Owner shall have the first refusal to purchase any unit or units which an Owner may desire to sell.

5. Expenses.

Each Owner shall pay his proper share of the expenses of the Syndicate, including organizational, legal, accounting, board, advertising, veterinary, etc., proportionate to the number of units which he holds. Bills will be sent out monthly and are payable within ten days.

6. Liability of Manager.

The Syndicate Manager shall not be personally liable for any act or omission committed by her except for willful misconduct or gross negligence.

7. Insurance.

The Syndicate Manager shall be responsible for insuring the horse. The expense of the insurance shall be shared by the Partners in accordance with this agreement.

8. Accounting.

The Syndicate Manager shall furnish each Partner periodically with a statement showing the receipts and expenditures and such other information as she may deem pertinent.

9. Special Meetings.

A special meeting of the Partner(s) may be called by either Partner at any time of mutual convenience with reasonable notice.

10. Active Participation.

Notwithstanding Manager's duties, each Partner shall materially and substantially participate in the day-to-day decisions affecting and relating to this joint venture and all management decisions relating to said horse.

11. Notices.

All required notices shall be effective and binding if sent by prepaid registered mail, telegram, cable, or delivered in person to the address of the respective Owners set out in the Schedule attached. Such address changes shall hereafter be designated in writing to the Syndicate Manager, addressed to:__Nancy Rider, Fireplace Road, East Hampton, New York 11937_____.

12. Miscellaneous.

This Agreement, when executed by the Owners, shall constitute the agreement between the parties, and shall be binding upon the Owners, their heirs, and assigns.

13. Liability.

This Agreement shall not be deemed to create any relationship by reason of which any party might be held liable for the omission or commission of any other party, unless otherwise provided.

14. Termination.

This Syndicate terminates on the sale of the horse at which time the Syndicate Manager shall furnish each Partner with an accounting. All income and expenses shall be shared in accordance with the proportionate ownership of units.

IN WITNESS WHEREOF we have executed this Agreement the day and date first above written.

_____

Signature

_____

Address

_____

Units Purchased

_____

Signature

_____

Address

_____

Units Purchased

Discussion of Syndicate Form

The agreement begins with the date and a brief introduction. The section called "Recitals" states the purpose of the syndicate to purchase a show horse, named Hope and Glory. The horse is described briefly.

1. Next, the financial terms are stated. The purchase price of the horse is broken into ten units, at $6,250 per unit. In this example, there are two members of the syndicate, so each member buys five units. The purpose of this agreement is to buy one horse with the selling price already set. The scope and purpose of the syndicate will determine the cost per unit.

2. The location sets the stabling arrangement for the horse under the auspices of the manager.

3. The manager is given full control of all horse-related decisions subject to the approval of the owner(s). In this case, the manager is one of the members of the syndicate, but in any event she is expected to make her best effort and to act in good faith.

4. If one of the owners wants to sell, the other owner has the first option to buy out her units.

5. Each owner pays his proportionate share of all expenses and bills are payable on a prompt basis.

6. The liability section is important since the manager cannot be sued for any damage to the horse unless she purposely committed an act of misconduct endangering the horse.

7. The manager must maintain insurance on the horse. She could be liable for the loss of the horse under Clause 6 if she purposely allows the policy to lapse.

8. The expenses and income of the syndicate must be regularly documented and mailed to the other owner(s).

9. Either owner can call a special meeting at a time and place convenient to both.

10. Each owner pledges to contribute substantial time to the daily business decisions. This section can be omitted, since the manager may realistically be responsible for most of the operation. The other owner here anticipated losses and wanted to provide for active participation under the tax law. The words alone will not ensure the tax outcome under the interpretation of the Revenue Service. (See "Material Participation Rules" under Partnership.)

11. All notices of meetings or other correspondence are binding if sent by registered mail, cabled, or hand delivered. Any address changes must be sent to the manager in writing.

12. The agreement represents all the terms. No one can complain later that there were oral additions to the writing and it is binding on any future parties with an interest in the syndicate.

13. Neither party is liable to the other for something not stated within this agreement.

14. The syndicate is no longer in existence once the horse is sold. At the point of the sale, the proceeds are split in proportion to the ownership interest.

Finally, the agreement is signed with the addresses and units purchased stated. This agreement does not take into account the complexity of appraising units or the method of calculating each owner's account. Any syndicate with more members or greater complexity would require professional advice, but a blank copy of this form is included as a model in the appendix.

CORPORATION

In the regular corporation, the skill and managerial expertise are provided by the paid employees of the corporation who may or may not own any stock. This is a more expensive and complicated way of doing business. Unlike proprietorships and partnerships, the corporation itself is a tax-paying entity; the corporation pays taxes on its profits. When profits are distributed to shareholders, the shareholders pay an additional tax based on their individual tax bracket. The corporate stockholders, like the limited partners, can be held liable for no more than their original investment; there is no personal liability for business losses, debts, negligence, and other similar items. At its most sophisticated levels, stocks of horse-racing farms have been sold publicly and the organization is regulated by securities laws.

To incorporate, an individual must file the Articles of Incorporation with the state, costing approximately $40.00. At this point, the individuals involved in organizing the corporation usually transfer money or property to the newly formed corporation in exchange for stock of the corporation. The corporation begins business for tax purposes when it starts the activities for which it was organized. See sample form page 18.

Discussion of the Articles of Incorporation

The Articles that must be on file with the State are straight forward.

1. Name(s) of the person(s) who are forming the corporation with address and home state.

2. The name of the corporation.

3. The purpose of the corporation is set out in general terms.

4. The person who will be the resident agent is named for mailing purposes and is the contact within the state; e.g., to whom all paperwork is sent.

5. The total number of shares is stated. Usually, these shares are not given any set (or par) value.

6. The number of directors is established.

7. The directors for the first meeting are named.

8. The rights and limitations of the powers of the Board of Directors are listed. Usually, these are very broad because this group is the executive body of the corporation.

9. No shareholder is to receive special rights to acquire additional stock over and above the other shareholders.

Finally, the Articles are signed by the person(s) forming the corporation. Filing these Articles is a formality which establishes the Corporation as a tax-paying entity with its own separate identity.

SAMPLE

THE ARTICLES OF INCORPORATION

FIRST: I, <u> Sue Ellen Marder </u>, whose post office address is <u> 803 Fireplace Road,</u> <u>East Hampton, Maryland 21120 </u> being at least eighteen (18) years of age, hereby forms a corporation under and by virtue of the General Laws of the State of <u> Maryland </u>.

SECOND: The name of the corporation (hereinafter referred to as the "Corporation"); is _____ _____.

THIRD: The purpose for which the Corporation is formed are:

(1) To conduct a riding stable including a lesson program, a sales barn and to maintain a string of show horses for outside owners.

(2) To do anything permitted by the appropriate laws of the state.

FOURTH: The post office address of the principal office of the Corporation in this state is _____ _____. The name and post office address of the Resident Agent of the Corporation are _____ _____. Said Resident Agent resides in this state.

FIFTH: The total number of shares of capital stock which the Corporation has authority to issue is <u>100</u> shares of common stock, without par value.

SIXTH: The number of Directors of the Corporation shall be increased or decreased pursuant to the By-Laws of the Corporation, but shall not be fewer than three unless:

(1) there is no stock held but then no fewer than one; or

(2) if no fewer than the number of stockholders.

SEVENTH: The names of the directors who shall act until the first meeting are _____ _____.

EIGHTH: The following provisions define, limit, and regulate the powers of the Corporation, the directors and stockholders:

(1) The Board of Directors of the Corporation may issue stock.

(2) The Board of Directors may classify or reclassify unissued stock.

(3) The Corporation may amend its Charter to alter contract rights of any outstanding stock.

(4) [Any other specific right can be enumerated here.]

Any enumeration of rights is not meant to limit any powers conferred upon the Board of Directors under state statute now in force or in force in the future.

NINTH: Unless the Board of Directors states otherwise, no shareholder has special rights to buy, convert or in any other way to acquire stocks.

I sign these Articles of Incorporation this _____ day of _____, 19_____.

_____
Signature

S CORPORATION

The S Corporation provides the advantages of limited liability without problems of double taxation. It is a special type of corporation designed for the small business owner, and the same general procedures must be followed for creating the S corporation as are described for the corporation. In general, the S corporation may have no more than thirty-five shareholders and must file an election with the Internal Revenue Service within seventy-five days of doing business. Unlike the regular corporation, the income and losses pass through directly to the shareholders as they would in a partnership and are reported on their personal income tax returns. The active or passive nature of the income depends on each individual shareholder's involvement. The reason for electing to form a Subchapter S Corporation is to obtain the advantages of incorporation, but, at the same time, to have the tax advantages of a partnership. When the business shows losses in the early years, a Subchapter S Corporation can pass those losses through to the shareholders to be deducted against their income. If the business becomes profitable, the income of the corporation is not taxed both to the business and then to the individual.

The major disadvantage to setting up either an S Corporation or a regular corporation is the amount of effort and cost involved. Legal assistance is advised and the costs for incorporation with the organizational basics listed may range from $200 to $1,000. However, a person can shop around for reasonable fees. Any attorney hired, however, should have experience in this area, because there can be major tax consequences as a result of a decision to form a corporation.

SUMMARY

This chapter has attempted to focus on key characteristics of certain types of businesses and the types of contracts associated with them. It is impossible to generalize about the form best suited for a particular horse business because it depends on the exact circumstances of the business and the people involved. In general, however, the simpler the form used, the lower will be legal and accounting expenses. For instance, there are adverse tax consequences on the transfer of property from a corporation to a shareholder, and the termination of either kind of corporation can be expensive. A tax advisor is needed to analyze the advantages and disadvantages. The following list summarizes the main points of each way of doing business:

Sole Proprietorship

- one person only
- higher individual tax rates
- direct use of losses against personal income
- business can terminate at any time
- personal liability in the event of a lawsuit
- material participation rules unlikely to limit use of losses
- least expensive to set up and maintain
- easiest, simplest form

Partnership

- more than one person
- income taxed at individual rate only
- direct use of losses against personal income
- distribution of property or cash is not taxed
- easily liquidated
- personal liability for partners in the event of a lawsuit
- material participation rules unlikely to limit use of losses
- relatively simple form

Limited Partnership

- less complex than a corporation
- more than one person involved, with general partner(s) who run the business and limited partner(s) who invest
- income taxed at individual rate only
- distributions of property or cash are not taxed
- limited partners partially sheltered from personal liability
- material participation rules define losses as passive for all limited partners
- more complex form

Corporation

- taxed at two levels: corporate and individual
- any distribution of property or cash to shareholders is taxed
- some income accumulated at corporate level is not distributed
- personal liability of shareholders against debt, negligence, and other obligations of the business is limited
- lower tax rates for the corporation
- transferable units for estate-planning purposes
- expensive to establish and maintain
- losses may be used to offset other corporate profits
- complex form

S Corporation

- income must be distributed to shareholders
- pass through of losses and income taxed at individual level
- must file an election with IRS within seventy-five days
- easier to get appreciated property out of the corporation
- limited personal liability (same as corporation)
- individual tax rates apply
- provides transferable unit for estate planning purposes
- expensive to establish and maintain
- complex form

2

Appraisal

An appraisal is a statement establishing a horse's value if the horse were to be sold in the open market. A person who is considered an expert in the field of buying and selling horses makes an educated opinion on the worth of a horse.

Example: There are times when a horse owner may choose for various reasons to donate his or her horse to a charitable institution that is a nonprofit organization registered with the Internal Revenue Service. The owner wishes to receive tax credit for making a charitable donation, and, therefore, needs to know the value of the horse. (The tax consequences are discussed in *Tax Planning and Preparation for Horse Owners,* Breakthrough, 1991.

A copy of the appraisal will be given to the organization with the horse and will be attached to the owner's tax return. A qualified stable owner or someone who regularly buys and sells horses, for example, may be asked to make such an appraisal. In any case, a general idea of the form is helpful.

In the sample appraisal that follows, the horse was a relatively young horse that had not been shown or hunted. The appraiser was not previously familiar with this horse but was asked by the college to conduct an appraisal for a prospective donor.

APPRAISAL OF A YOUNG HORSE NEVER SHOWN

I am qualified to appraise the value of a horse in today's market. I have been buying and selling show hunters for the last twenty-five years and am considered an expert in the field.

I have personally evaluated the horse described as follows within the last ____Ten____ (__10__) days:

Name: Cold Sassy Tree

Age: 7

Breed: Appaloosa/Thoroughbred cross

Sex: Gelding

Size: 16 h 2"

This horse is owned by ____Robert E, Lee____ residing at ____26100 Yohoe Road,____ Hereford, Maryland ____ and said horse is being donated to ____Goucher College of____ Towson, Maryland ____. Based on the soundness, size, disposition and athletic ability of this horse, I would set the fair market value at ____Nine Thousand Five Hundred____ Dollars ($_9,500.00____). This price is fair and reasonable given the market and demand for horses of this type.

This appraisal price is an objective estimate to the best of my ability and knowledge on this _____ day of _____, 19 _____.

_____
Signature of Appraiser

Discussion

In the first paragraph, the appraiser establishes her credentials by stating the number of years she had been in the business and in what capacity. Next, the horse is described and the owner is identified with his address. Finally and most importantly, the appraiser states the basis of the appraisal price and sets an exact figure to the best of her knowledge. Obviously, the worth of a horse is highly subjective and speculative, but the appraiser may be subject to prosecution if she purposely misstates the value of the horse. Then she signs and dates the document.

Paragraph 1 - state your credentials as an expert in the horse business for the type of horse being appraised.

Paragraphs 2 and 3 - state the name and address of the donor, the place of donation if known, and a full description of the horse.

Follow with the basis of the appraisal and the monetary fair market value of the horse to the best of your knowledge.

The basis of the appraisal is a recent first hand observation of the horse, considering external factors such as show record, winnings, or breeding potential in today's market. As real estate appraisers do with houses, you might use comparable horses and their selling prices as an evaluative tool.

Owners will often tell the appraiser what they paid for the horse or the additional amounts they have invested in the horse. Often these figures are not very reliable guidelines in the appraisal process because commonly a horse is not worth its purchase price (another sad reality of the horse business).

Finally, the form is dated and signed.

3

Bill of Sale

A bill of sale is a document signed by the seller stating that he or she received a certain amount of money in exchange for a horse. The seller acknowledges that the money was received and the horse was sold to the buyer named. The bill of sale serves as proof of ownership for the buyer and provides a statement that the seller has been paid in full. If a horse is sold at a profit, there is a potential tax liability. On audit, the Internal Revenue Service may ask to see the bill of sale.

When purchasing a horse, the buyer should always get a bill of sale warranting ownership and stating the seller's address. All official registration should be transferred at the time of the sale. That way you avoid the sad case of the person who buys a thoroughbred, but never receives the papers or a bill of sale. He or she is always told "it is in the mail," and eight months later the buyer is contacted by the real owner who is not the person who sold the horse. The real owner sues the buyer for the return of the horse. After six more months, the buyer loses the horse to the owner, but is reimbursed for the board bills. The buyer must track down the seller and enforce a judgment for the purchase price against the fraudulent seller who has no job and no money. Buyer suffers heartbreak and the loss of the purchase price.

> **Example:** Judy has finally talked her parents into buying her a horse. They find a suitable pony for Pony Club events. Dad writes a check for One Thousand Dollars to Friendly Neighbor and Judy rides the pony home. He receives the following bill of sale (page 26).

Discussion

This is a simple and direct bill of sale. "I," the person selling, followed by an address, states how much money was paid and by whom and who lives where. Next, the horse is described. The seller promises he is the owner and had the right to sell and will defend against any claims to the contrary. The form is then executed with a signature and dated.

A more complex bill of sale may be necessary if the horse is very expensive and the owner is making additional warranties as to the horse's breeding record, show winnings, or suitability for a particular purpose, or, for the case where a mare is sold in foal to a particular stallion, with a breeding certificate attached. (See Chapter 6, Purchase Agreement.)

SAMPLE

BILL OF SALE

I, _____Friendly Neighbor_____, residing at _____715 Maisemore Road,_____
Parkton, Maryland_____ in consideration of _One Thousand_
Dollars_____, hereby paid to me by _____Dear Dad_____,
residing at _____612 Bunk Hill Road, Parkton, Maryland_____, sell to
Dear Dad_____ the following described horse:

Name: Sassy

Age: 8

Color: Chestnut

Breed: Welsh Cross (no papers)

Sex: Mare

Size: 11 h 2"

    I hereby covenant that I am the lawful owner of the horse; that I have the right to sell the horse; and that I will warrant and defend said horse against lawful claims and demands of all persons.
Executed this _____4th_____ day of _____July_____, 19 _9_ .

_____
Signature of Seller

4

Consignment Agreement for Sale of Horse and Limited Power of Attorney

In a consignment agreement, an owner entrusts his horse to another person whose job is to sell the horse. Thus, instead of finding a buyer himself, the seller signs a contract with a middleman who handles the sale. In most consignment agreements, the owner sends the horse to the barn of the salesperson, the consignment stable.

The person who takes the horse on consignment is acting as an agent for the owner. He or she is given the authority to sign a bill of sale and collect money for the owner through a second agreement, called a limited power of attorney. It is called a limited power of attorney because the power of the agent to act in place of the owner is limited to this horse transaction and to the specific terms of this agreement.

Example: Jeannette Labbat owns a big quarterhorse mare, but it is not suitable for her in the adult division. She decides to send the horse to a local professional to be sold. She is familiar with the excellent quality of this sales stable and has personally inspected the stables and turnout facilities. She has also spoken with satisfied customers who have sold their horses through this agent.

She paid five thousand dollars ($5,000) for the mare and wants to sell her for that. She knows the horse is a hardkeeper and requires special feeding. The mare is temperamental so that she does not want her transferred to other barns before money changes hands. She has heard that some horses have been sold while under medication unbeknownst to the buyer. These are all concerns she wants to address in the contract.

Jeannette should prepare a consignment agreement with a limited power of attorney as a separate form. Also, she needs an agreement authorizing the consignee to act as an agent in this sale. The consignee needs a power of attorney that will be attached as a separate contract.

CONSIGNMENT AGREEMENT

THIS AGREEMENT is made between ___Jeannette Labbat___, the "Consignor", residing at ___Sellers Landing, New York___, and ___Ralph Maristo___, the "Consignee", residing at ___Speonk, New York___.

1. Description
The Consignor owns a horse described in this section below:

    (a) Name: Saddle Deck

    (b) Age: 10

    (c) Breed: Quarterhorse

    (d) Sex: Mare

    (e) Size: 17 hards

2. Purpose
The Consignor is in the business of buying and selling horses as an agent. The Consignor desires to sell said horse. Consignee agrees to make his best effort to sell said horse on behalf of the Consignor.

3. Warranties
The Consignee accepts said horse into his sales barn under the following terms:

    (a) The minimum selling price for the horse is Five Thousand ($5,000.00) Dollars unless changed in writing by the Consignor before a sale.

    (b) The horse will not be released on trial without Consignor's written consent.

    (c) The horse will not be used for lesson, show or lease purposes while under this consignment agreement without Consignor's written consent.

    (d) The Consignor will not ride the horse while under this Agreement.

4. Board
In consideration of ___$550.00___ per horse per month paid by Consignor in advance on the first day of each month, the Consignee agrees to board said horse until sold or this Agreement is terminated.

5. Commission
At the sale of said horse, the Consignee shall receive a commission of ___10___% on all funds received. The Consignor shall receive the balance of all funds on the sale of said horse within 10 days. The Consignee shall charge ___1/2___% late fee per month on any late payment.

6. Care of Horse

(a) The Consignee agrees to provide normal and reasonable care to maintain the health and well-being of said horse. This care includes (i) _____ daily grooming _____, (ii) _blanketing when necessary_, and (iii) _____ daily individual _____ turnout for brief periods ,

(b) Routine veterinary and farrier care are authorized with direct billing. Any extraordinary care requires the consent of the Consignor unless on an emergency basis.

(c) The following feed and supplements shall be fed daily:

Hay: 5 large flakes   2 times daily
Grain: 6 lbs.   2 times daily
Daily supplements:
     Biotin
     Mirra Coat
     Electrolytes

(d) Exercise

Said horse shall be ridden or lunged by Consignee or a competent rider employed by Consignee at least _four_ days a week.

The Consignee will show the horse to potential buyers under the following terms.

(1) Said horse does not leave the grounds of the Consignee.

(2) The horse is not ridden by potential buyers more than twice a day.

(3) The horse is not medicated for any exercise or presentation to buyers.

7. Assumption of Risk at Sale

The Buyer takes possession only upon transfer of full consideration to Consignee. The risk of loss passes to Buyer at the Consignee's farm upon delivery of any relevant registration papers and a bill of sale. Buyer assumes all costs at the point of said transfer and prior to the horse's release from Consignee's premises.

None of the above terms are subject to change without explicit written agreement by the Consignor.

8. Lien

Consignee agrees to keep horse free and clear of all liens and encumbrances.

9. Attorney's Fees

This Agreement is terminated upon a breach of any material term and the wronged party has the right to collect all reasonable fees and costs from the breaching party.

10. Termination

Either party may cancel this agreement prior to sale on _____ five _____ days written notice and final accounting thereto.

11. Governing Law

In all respects, this Agreement shall be constructed in accordance with and governed by the laws of the State of _____ New York _____.

Dated   Signature of Consignor

Dated   Signature of Consignee

Discussion of Consignment Agreement

Once the client, Jeannette, is personally satisfied with this sales barn, she is the one to provide the agreement.

1. In the first section, both parties are named with addresses given, and the horse is described. If a horse has any other distinguishing features, these might be included.

2. The purpose of the agreement is stated. The seller, Jeannette, is the consignor and she is sending her horse to a sales agent, the consignee, who will make his best efforts to sell her horse.

3. (a) This is the minimum price the owner is willing to accept for the horse. (They may agree to ask more at first.) This term is very important. Jeannette may reduce this figure in writing or, under the more optimistic circumstances, raise it, but only if a sale has not been consummated.

    (b) In the following paragraphs, there are blank spaces for any other specific terms required by either party:
Here Jeannette does not want this horse to be moved to another barn for a trial period before the sale (a requisite of many buyers in a buyer's market). She may have to change this provision later.

    (c) The horse is not available for purposes other than sale, e.g., lessons, show, or lease. The owner should recognize that some sales barns also function as lesson stables where the board is reduced if the horse is used in lessons. Sometimes these lessons can lead to a sale to a rider in the barn. Showing does give the horse exposure and leasing reduces costs. On the other hand, Jeannette must weigh the advantages against the inherent risks of injury. If she does allow the horse to be used in lessons, she needs the indemnity paragraph from the Lease Agreement. Whichever route is chosen, the terms must be explicitly stated.

    (d) The last term is included by the consignee. He may find that owners show up at inopportune times to ride their horses when he has clients lined up. Some owners are poor riders who are detriments to the sale of their own horses. They are also not emotionally detached about the sale of their horses. Whatever the agent's policy, the rules must be clarified.

4. The cost of board is set. The horse continues to eat until he is sold. The consignee rarely fronts the costs until the time of sale. He needs the monthly payments.

5. The amount of commission on the sales price is established. Some agents set a sales price over and above the owner's price and collect the difference as profit. This practice can lead to inflated sales prices if the owner does not understand that this will be the case. Whatever the practice, Jeannette needs to get this in writing.
The consignor should receive the sales money promptly with a late charge as penalty.

6. The care of the horse is clarified.
It is important to inspect the facility before entrusting the horse to the sales agent or anyone connected with the barn.

    (a) Once satisfied with the place, Jeannette may still specify the daily care. This section protects the agent also, because he can stipulate what care is included in his base price. (See Chapter 12, Stable Record Form.) Because the owner is often not there on a regular basis, grooming and daily care are necessary for sales purposes.

    (b) Routine veterinary and farrier care are provided with direct billing. Emergency care is authorized until the owner can be notified.

(c) Feeding schedules and supplements are of assistance to the consignee who, like the owner, wants the horse well-maintained. There may be additional fees in this section to cover the supplements or special feeding.

(d) Exercise can be specified as to number of times per week or can be left more open. The rider is also generally designated as an employee of the barn.

7. The risk of the horse's death or injury passes to the buyer while the horse is still at the consignee's barn, once the buyer has paid in full and has received the relevant paperwork. This may include thoroughbred papers, a bill of sale, or any other formal registration. The buyer assumes all costs at this point and arranges for delivery. If the horse dies before he leaves the consignee's barn, the buyer still owns the horse and is not entitled to a refund.

It is possible to sell on an installment, but the owner/consignor must consent in writing. Secondly, the consignee may take his entire commission at the time of the sale. These details require additional terms. (See Chapter 5 and the Promissory Note form.)

8. Even the most established stables have been known to declare bankruptcy. The horses owned by the consignee become the property of the bank or creditors and may be sold at auction. This section provides that the consigned horse is kept free and clear of any financial obligations of the consignee. The ownership should never be signed over to the consignee even with an explicit understanding that the agent is only "pretending" to be the owner.

9. If either party does not abide by the agreement, the other person may terminate the agreement. If the disagreement cannot be resolved, the person who broke the agreement is responsible for reasonable attorney's fees and court costs.

10. This section allows Jeannette to change her mind about selling, or she may move the horse after giving five days notice. Sometimes an agent recognizes that he can't sell the horse and recommends a different location for the horse. They both have this flexibility.

11. In the final section, the controlling state is named. Different states have different laws. A consignee might live in New Jersey but ride in Connecticut. The consignee's residence may be New York.

Finally, the agreement is signed and dated. Remember, there must be signatures or no agreement exists.

SAMPLE

LIMITED POWER OF ATTORNEY

I, _____Jeanette Labbot_____, of _____Sellers Landing, New York_____, do hereby execute this Limited Power of Attorney with the intention that the attorney-in-fact hereinafter named shall be able to act in my place for the purposes set forth herein.

SECTION 1. Designation of Attorney.

I constitute and appoint ___Ralph Maristo___ to be my attorney-in-fact to act for me, in my name, and in my place.

SECTION 2. Effective Date of Power of Attorney.

2.01 This Limited Power of Attorney shall be effective as of the date of its execution by me, and shall remain effective unless same revoked by me, until midnight on _____.

2.02 This Limited Power of Attorney shall not be affected by my disability, it being my specific intention that my attorney-in-fact shall continue to act as such even though I may not be competent to ratify the actions of my attorney-in-fact.

SECTION 3. Powers.

3.01 My attorney-in-fact shall have all of the powers, discretions, elections, and authorities granted by statute, common law, and under any rule of court necessary to sell my _10 year old, 17 hand quarterhorse mare named ``Saddle Deck'' for a price of at least $5,000.00_. In addition thereto, and not in limitation thereof, my attorney-in-fact shall also have the power set forth below.

3.02 My attorney-in-fact may collect and receive, with or without the institution of suit or other legal process, all debts, monies, objects, interest, and demands due to me pursuant to the aforementioned sale.

3.03 My attorney-in-fact may endorse my name for deposit into a savings, checking, or money-market account of mine with respect to sums payable to me pursuant to the aforementioned sale.

3.04 My attorney-in-fact may execute, seal, acknowledge, and deliver any documents necessary, advisable or expedient with respect to the aforementioned sale.

SECTION 4. Ratification.

4.01 I hereby ratify, allow, acknowledge, and hold firm and valid all acts heretofore or hereafter taken by my attorney-in-fact by virtue of these presents in connection with the aforementioned contract.

AS WITNESS my hand and seal this _____ day of _____, 19_____.

WITNESS:

_____

_____

_____
Jeannette Labbot   (SEAL)

Discussion of Limited Power of Attorney

The agent, here Mr. Maristo, needs a power of attorney from Jeannette to sell the horse. Once this form is executed, he will be acting as an authorized agent, a kind of owner-replacement, just for the purpose of this sale.

1. First, the consignor, Jeannette, is named with her address and her intent to authorize Mr. Maristo as her agent.

2. She sets the term of the agreement, unless revoked sooner. She also provides for his on-going authority over the contract in the event she suffers a disability, i.e., coma, or is declared mentally incompetent by the court.

3. Thirdly, she confers all powers necessary to sell the horse as named and described for the agreed upon price. The agent may collect all fees due and handle all financial aspects of the sale, including deposits at the bank.

If any papers must be signed, he may write his signature as agent for the owner and deliver all necessary documents.

4. Finally, Jeannette states that she will stand behind all acts of the agent within the scope of this agreement. Then she dates and signs with a person witnessing the signature. The word "seal" is a formality.

This power of attorney will be executed at the time of the Consignment Agreement.

5

Installment Sale
and
Promissory Note

In an installment sale, the seller does not receive all the money at the time of the sale. For the installment sale described in this chapter, the seller signs a bill of sale stating he received a down payment plus a promissory note in payment for the purchase of the horse. A promissory note is an "I Owe You," in which the person who signs the note acknowledges that he owes money to someone else. The terms of the promissory note may vary. The amount owed may be payable on the demand of the person who holds the note or it may include a payment schedule.

The bill of sale and the promissory note are the two parts of this installment sale.

THE INSTALLMENT SALE

Example: Tony promises to buy his fiancee a horse named Tax Practice, but he does not have the ready cash for such a generous gift. Tony does have Two Thousand Five Hundred Dollars ($2,500.00) for a down payment, and he could make regular payments at intervals. The seller, Jane, does not want to lose the sale but worries about releasing the horse without a guarantee that her money will be paid. For example, she does not want Tony to cease making payments or return the horse to her already-crowded barn if he breaks up with his fiancee.

The solution is to create a bill of sale transferring ownership of the horse to Tony in exchange for a down payment and a promissory note with a payment schedule. Keep in mind, however, that if the horse dies or is injured, Tony still owes on the note. In this case, the buyer (Tony) is wise to insure a horse bought on credit. If the horse were to die or be humanely destroyed, the insurance would cover what he still owed and the seller is assured the buyer will have the money to finish paying for the horse even if the collateral dies.

The installment sale requires a bill of sale specifically stating the receipt of the cash plus the promissory note as payment. The promissory note states the actual terms of the payment.

SAMPLE

BILL OF SALE
WITH PROMISSORY NOTE

THIS BILL OF SALE, made this _____, day of _____December, 1990_____, by and between _____JANE O'BRIEN_____, hereinafter called Seller, and _____TONY_____ WINNER_____ hereinafter called Buyer.

   1. That in consideration of the payment of _____Seven Thousand Five Hundred_____, Dollars ($7,500.00), Two Thousand Five Hundred Dollars ($2,500.00) in cash and a _____Five Thousand Dollars ($5,000.00)_____ promissory note, by the Buyer to the Seller, the receipt of which is hereby acknowledged, said Seller does hereby bargain, sell, transfer, assign and convey unto said Buyer, its successors and assigns, free and clear of all debts, liens and encumbrances, the horse as described below:

A. Name: Tax Practice

B. Age: 4

C. Color: Chestnut

D. Breed: unreg. t.b.

E. Sex: Gelding

F. Size: 17 h.

   2. The Seller hereby represents that said horse hereby sold is his/her horse and that title is vested and that it has a good and perfect right to sell same, and that no debts, claims, obligations or encumbrances exist on or against said horse.

   WITNESS, the hands of the Seller and Buyer.

WITNESS:

_____

_____
JANE O'BRIEN

_____
Address

_____
Telephone

_____
TONY WINNER

_____
Address

_____
Telephone

36

Discussion of Installment Bill of Sale

Like a regular bill of sale, this sale states the name of the two parties. If either is a corporation, the words, "a corporation", and the state of incorporation should follow.

Next, the consideration is stated, that is, the total price followed by how much was paid in cash and how much was paid by a promissory note. The seller claims she is transferring the horse free and clear with no debts attached for the horse which is described. The pronoun "it" is used to avoid confusion with "he" or "she".

Then the seller states that she completely owns the horse and has the right to sell it. Both parties sign, with addresses and phone numbers. There is a space for witnesses to assure the verity of the signatures. Witnesses are not always required, but may prevent any denials in the future. In any event, they are always a good safeguard in any contract.

THE PROMISSORY NOTE

The agreement is made between Tony and Jane. Tony buys the horse from Jane for $2,500.00 in cash and a $5,000.00 balance. This note covers the balance. Without this note, the seller's alternative would be to retain an interest in the horse. When a person borrows money from a bank to buy a car, the bank records a lien on the car until the loan is fully repaid. In essence, the same procedure is followed when a horse is sold on the installment basis. Yet, the situation is more complex, because horses are easily injured. A person might sell a horse for fifty thousand dollars but, within the year, the horse's resale value could drop to twenty thousand, or less because of injury.

With a promissory note, the seller is in a much more secure position than with a lien on the horse.

SAMPLE

PROMISSORY NOTE

THIS AGREEMENT is made between _____Tony Winner_____

(the ''Undersigned'') and _____Jane O'Brien_____

1. Consideration

FOR VALUE RECEIVED, __TONY__ __WINNER_____ does hereby promise to pay to the order of ____JANE____ __O'BRIEN_____ the sum of __Five__ __Thousand__ Dollars ($__5,000.00__), together with interest on the unpaid principal balance at the rate of ____Ten____ Percent (__10__%) per annum from the date hereof in installments beginning on _____ _____ and on the first of each month thereafter in the amount of $__106.24__ until the entire principal balance is paid in full or until __sixty (60) months__ thereafter, at which time the amount then owing shall be due.

2. Payment Terms

The monthly payments are calculated on an amortization schedule of ____five____ years and the full amount then owing shall be due ____five____ years from the date of the first payment, unless otherwise accelerated under the terms and conditions hereof. Both principal and interest shall be payable at the address of __JANE O'BRIEN_____ at __Fireplace Road, East Hampton, New York 11937_____, or at such other address as may be designated from time to time by written notification to the Undersigned by the holder hereof.

3. Prepayment

The Undersigned shall have the right to prepay, at any time or times, without penalty, all or any part of the balance of the principal hereof. Any such prepayment shall be applied first to any unpaid interest accrued hereunder and then to the principal, in which case the amounts due with respect to succeeding interest payments hereunder shall be adjusted accordingly.

4. Default

In the event (any of which events shall be deemed an ''event of default''): (a) the Undersigned shall fail to make any payment of principal or interest when due hereunder and such failure shall have continued for ten (10) days after written notice of such default by the holder hereof, or (b) any voluntary petition by, or involuntary petition against, the Undersigned shall be filed under any chapter of the Federal Bankruptcy Act, or any proceeding involving the Undersigned shall be instituted under any other law relating to the relief of debtors, and such petition or proceeding shall not be vacated within ten (10) days thereafter, or (c) the Undersigned shall make any assignment for the benefit of creditors, or (d) a judgment shall be entered against the Undersigned in any court of record and shall not be satisfied within five (5) days thereafter, then the holder hereof, in his, his/her or their sole discretion may declare this Promissory Note to be due forthwith, and the same shall thereupon become immediately due and payable in full, all without any presentment, demand or notice of any kind, which are hereby waived.

5. Rights of Holder

No delay or omission on the part of the holder hereof in the exercise of any right or remedy shall operate as a waiver thereof, and no single or partial exercise by the holder of any right or remedy shall preclude other or further exercise of any right or remedy.

6. Remedies

The Undersigned hereby authorizes any attorney of any court within the State of __Maryland_____ or elsewhere to confess judgment against the Undersigned at any time after this Promissory Note is due (whether upon normal maturity or acceleration hereunder), hereby waiving all exemptions, for the principal amount of this Promissory Note and interest and attorney's fees and court costs. If this Promissory Note is referred to an attorney for collection, then there shall be added to the amount due and owing hereunder reasonable attorney's fees of not less than 15% or such amount as any Court in which an action is filed deems to be reasonable, plus costs of collection.

7. Waiving of Defenses

The Undersigned hereby waives presentment, demand, notice of dishonor, protest and all other demands and notices whatsoever in connection with the delivery, acceptance, performance and enforcement of this Note.

Executed this _____ day of _____, 19_____.

_____
TONY WINNER
_____
Address
_____

_____
Telephone

Discussion of Promissory Note

First, the note is dated and the parties are named.

1. This section states the amount this note is worth. It is like a check "pay to the order of," and it is equally negotiable. It could be endorsed over to someone else to collect on it. If the seller needed cash now, he could sell the note at a discounted price.

2. The payments begin on a specified date for a specified number of months with the amount of the monthly payment stated. The address of the payee is also included subject to change. The payee may move or transfer the note to another person.

3. This section allows prepayment at anytime with the order of application, first to interest and then principal.

4. If Tony doesn't pay as scheduled and receives written notice from Jane, he has ten days to pay the installment, or Jane can declare the note immediately due. Furthermore, the note is immediately due if Tony declares bankruptcy, applies for any other legal protection, or does not seem able to pay on this note as specified and does not prove otherwise within the number of days stated.

5. No matter what Jane, the holder of this note, does, Tony still owes the money. If she dies, he owes the money to her legatee.

6. In this section, Tony agrees that Jane's attorney has the right to collect the payment if overdue and Tony will be liable for any additional costs necessary to collect on this note.

7. Tony relinquishes any right to use defenses to avoid paying this note. For example, he can't claim the horse isn't worth the money.

Finally, the note is dated and signed, and completed with the address and telephone number of the person who owes the money.

6

Purchase Agreement

A purchase agreement is a contract in which the buyer has made a down payment. The seller and buyer both agree to the terms of the sale and agree on the date of the closing when the purchase price will be paid in full and the ownership of the horse will be transferred to the buyer.

Example: George Foran buys an expensive show pony. He will pay in full before delivery but makes a down payment to the owner to hold the horse for him. He wants to be certain that the purchase price will not be changed between the time the deposit is made and the pay off. He also needs assurance that the pony will not be sold to anyone else, and that the seller is responsible for the pony until the payment is made in full, in two weeks time. Additionally, if the pony were to die in the meantime, George wants his down payment refunded. George prepares a purchase agreement.

SAMPLE

PURCHASE AGREEMENT

THIS AGREEMENT is made between ___George Foran___, residing at ___Bridgehampton, New York___ ("Buyer") and ___Abin Hopping___, residing at ___Bridgehampton, New York___ ("Seller") for the purchase described below:

Name: ___Flower Pot___

Age: ___10___

Color: ___Bay___

Breed: ___Anglo Arab___

Sex: ___Mare___

Size: ___14 h 2"___

1. Purchase Price
For the total sum of $___50,000.00___, Seller agrees to sell and Buyer agrees to buy said horse based on the terms to follow.

2. Payment Terms
The Buyer agrees to pay $___10,000.00___, as a deposit on ___the execution of this Agreement___ and the balance due of $___40,000.00___ on ___the day of delivery, no more than 14 days from now___.

3. Warranties
   (a) Seller covenants that he/she is the lawful owner of said horse; that he/she has the right to sell said horse; and that he will warrant and defend the horse against lawful claims and demands of all persons.
   (b) Seller makes no other promises, express or implied, including the warranties of fitness for a particular purpose unless further provided in this Agreement.
   (c) Seller warrants the following: ___this horse is qualified for the Devon Horse Show and has a permanent size pony card.___
   (d) Buyer waives any claim for damage should said horse fail to meet the above warranties at the time of delivery, unless such defect is discovered within ___ten (10)___ days from delivery to Buyer.

4. Transfer of Ownership
Once Seller has received payment in full, Seller shall transfer all owner and registration papers of the horse at his own expense.

5. Risk of Loss
Seller assumes all risk of loss until the Buyer takes delivery or until the Buyer begins transfer of the horse, whichever comes first.

6. Law

The terms of this Agreement shall be governed by the laws of the State of _____Maryland_____.

7. Breach

Either party may nullify this Agreement if the other party breaches a material term of this Agreement. The wronged party may recover reasonable attorney's fees and court costs.

Executed this _____ day of _____, 19_____.

SELLER: BUYER:

_____   _____

Signature   Signature

_____   _____

Address   Address

Discussion

Again, I stress the importance of getting the names, addresses and description of the horse. The age and size of the horse are material because show horses or ponies are often bought for their size in certain hunter divisions. Age is another significant factor because a horse described as a ten-year-old may have a different value as a sixteen-year-old.

1. The purchase price must be clearly set here. There have been cases in which sudden interest is sparked in a horse because of winnings or breeding, and a seller may be tempted to raise the price after the contract has been signed.

2. To protect the seller, the payment terms ensure that a cash transaction does not drag out to become an unintended installment sale.

3. This section of warranties is one of the most sensitive areas.
- **(a)** The seller states that he owns the horse and has the right to sell it. This is a crucial protection to the buyer.
- **(b)** On the other hand, the seller protects himself by saying "what you see is what you get" with the emphasis on nothing more. In other words, "buyer beware" is the basic premise.
- **(c)** If the seller does include any assurances as to soundness or suitability, these are explicitly listed. The buyer may require a written statement of the facts he is relying on as the basis of this purchase, in this case the qualification for the Devon Horse Show and the size of the pony.
- **(d)** The ten-day period is not a trial of the horse. The contract will be void only if the buyer or seller has not fulfilled his part of the bargain.

4. The owner is responsible for transferring papers and any necessary notices to the buyer.

5. The risk of losing the horse is assumed by the buyer as soon as he takes delivery. The actual point of delivery can vary. If the buyer boards where he bought the horse, this date would begin when payment is made in full. If the seller delivers the horse, the risk passes when the horse arrives on the buyer's farm or when the buyer himself picks up the horse with his van or his agent's van.

6. George can declare this agreement null and void if the seller breaks a material term of the agreement. The court and attorney's costs are paid for by the seller if the buyer is forced into court to get his money refunded.

The contract has no validity until both parties have signed.

7

Lease

A lease is a contract in which a person pays for the use of a horse over a set period. The person who leases the horse assumes the responsibilities of the horse as if he or she owned it under the terms of the agreement.

Leasing high-quality horses has become a popular alternative to the high cost of purchasing.

Example: Norma wants to lease a junior hunter from Karen Halsey for her grandson, Fred. Fred is sixteen years old and hopes to qualify for the indoor shows in the fall, so Norma wants to be able to renew the lease for his last junior year. Unless he renews, she wants the lease to end after the National in November. She does not have a lump sum to pay the lease fee, but would like the payments spread out over the year. The horse Norma wants has shown in the working hunter division for the last few years, and she knows the owner wants to reduce the pounding on the horse's legs, so she is willing to agree the horse will not be shown in any division requiring it to jump higher than 3'6". Norma also is sensitive to special care requests by the owner, and is willing to take out insurance to cover the horse's value if he dies during the lease period. She also would like the opportunity to buy the horse in the event Fred is successful. The following lease meets her concerns.

SAMPLE

LEASE AGREEMENT

This Lease is made ____September, 199____ between ____Tynne Birch____
residing at ____West Lane, Pound Ridge, New York____, (hereinafter
referred to as "Lessor" and ____Norma Edwards____, residing on ____Fireplace Road,
East Hampton, New York____, (hereinafter referred to as "Lessee").

1. Term
The term of this Lease shall be for a period beginning ____January 1, 199____
and ending no later than ____December 1, 199____, or as otherwise provided for
herein:

2. Description
This Lease covers the horse(s) described in this section below.

A. Name: Tax Practice

B. Age: 10

C. Breed: Thoroughbred (no papers)

D. Sex: Gelding

E. Size: 17 h

3. Consideration/Payment
Lessee shall pay a fee of ____Fifteen Thousand Dollars ($15,000.00)____,
payable as follows:

Payment	Date
$5,000.00	August 1, 199
$5,000.00	January 1, 199
$5,000.00	February 1, 199

4. Uses of Horse and Limitations
Lessee covenants not to use the horse for any purpose other than as set forth: __said horse
shall be shown in 3'6" hunter divisions and shall be ridden in lesson
and schooling sessions as necessary__.
Lessor promises that said horse is capable and suited for said purpose. Lessor explicitly denies
the right to any other party for any sublease agreement, barring all other riders except the Lessee's
instructor or chosen professional rider where appropriate.

5. Instructions for Care
Lessee will follow all practices consistent with quality care ____on the A horse show
circuit____ at Lessee's own expense. Lessee shall provide all necessary
veterinarian and blacksmith needs at Lessee's own expense. In addition said horse requires:

46

(a) a double stall when vanning

(b) shavings for bedding

(c) pads on front shoes

(d) daily turn-out alone when not showing

(Grain rations and hay plus stall size can be stated here.)

6. Risk of Loss and Insurance

(a) Lessee assumes risk of loss or injury to said horse(s), barring an act of the Lessor or Lessor's agent.

(b) Lessee shall at his/her own expense at all times during the term of this lease maintain in force a policy or policies of insurance written by one or more responsible insurance carriers acceptable to Lessor. A copy of said policy must be mailed to Lessor within a month of taking delivery.

The liability under such policy shall not be less than ___Fifty Thousand Dollars___ (\$50,000.00)___ payable to the Lessor as sole beneficiary.

7. Hold Harmless

Lessee agrees to hold Lessor harmless from any act of negligence of Lessee or any of his agents, contractors or employees, or arising from any accident, injury, or damage whatsoever however caused to any person or persons, or to the property of any person, persons, or corporations occurring during such term of this Lease and arising out of the use or care of said horse.

8. Ownership

Lessor warrants that he/she owns said horse free and clear and has the right to execute this Lease.

9. Options

(a) Lessee has the option to renew this Lease for an additional ___twelve___ (_12_) months if a request is made in writing ___sixty___ days prior to the expiration of this Lease, provided the horse is available for a lease.

(b) If horse is placed up for sale, the Lessee has the right of first refusal to purchase said horse within ___two___ (_2_) months of the expiration of said lease not to exceed ___Fifty Thousand Dollars (\$50,000.00)___.

10. Covenant Not to Encumber

Lessee agrees not to encumber said horse(s) with any lien, charge, or related claim and to hold Lessor harmless therefrom.

11. Default

Upon material breach of this Agreement, Lessor reserves the right to remove such horse without incurring any responsibility to Lessee.

This Agreement is terminated upon a breach of any material term and the other party has the right to collect all reasonable fees and costs from the breaching party.

Signed this _____ day of _____, 19_____.

LESSOR:

_____
Signature

_____
Address

_____
Telephone

LESSEE:

_____
Signature

_____
Address

_____
Telephone

Discussion

The beginning of the lease names the parties, sets the date the lease was drafted, and includes both addresses.

1.   The term of the lease sets the time span of the arrangement. A lease might cover a single horse show or run as long as several years. Because horses are prone to injuries or junior riders may need to upgrade their horses after a year, a show season or one year is the most common term.

2.   The description of the horse is a basic part of the agreement. If several horses are leased, for instance, for a summer camp or a lease for a school program, all the descriptions would be included here.

3.   This section clarifies the fee and the schedule of the payment. As noted, most of the money is generally due in the first half of the lease when the lessee needs the horse(s). The lessor can threaten to take the horse back if the payment is not made.

Horses or ponies suitable for local shows or hunting are sometimes available for "free leases." People are often looking for good homes for horses they don't want to sell. This way, they know the horse or pony is well maintained, but they don't have the monthly expense. The lessee pays all expenses, but there is no "lease fee." If this is the case, a $1.00 consideration as the lease fee is stated here.

4.   This section clarifies the scope of the horse's use under the lease. Here Norma agrees the horse, Tax Practice, will stay in the 3'6" jumping division.

Often an older horse is leased for a less demanding division. The owner/lessor has a vested interest that his ex-jumper be used exclusively for equitation or that his working hunter stay in the junior division. The horse is saved from the wear and tear of jumping more demanding courses.

The owner/lessor warrants in turn that the horse is sound as required for the division and suited for the purpose as represented. He may here deny the use of the horse by other riders. This lessor likes Fred's instructor and wants the horse to stay in the same barn where the care is excellent. She does not want the horse subleased to another stable.

5.   The "Instructions for Care" vary in specificity depending on past practices, the geographic area, and the purpose and quality of the lessee. Veterinary and blacksmith fees are included here at the lessee's expense. Sometimes a lessor will require a preapproval of the boarding facility. In this instance, where the horse is showing on the A circuit with a quality barn, the grain and hay rations are not specified. Norma is familiar with the stable management where Tax Practice will be boarding. The size of stall where applicable also can be included here. (See Chapter 12, Stable Record Form.)

Special instructions are listed, stating idiosyncracies or directions necessary to the horse's well-being; for example, he panics without a double stall when vanning, eats straw bedding, and needs pads because of flat feet.

6.   The "Risk of Loss and Insurance" Section is a protection for both parties. The lessee assumes the cost, and the premium is no more than 5% of the face value of the contract, so in this case, with a $50,000 horse, the policy adds an additional $2,500 to the cost of the lease.

For instance, a friend of Norma leased a horse that suffered a spontaneous fracture while turned out and was humanely destroyed under veterinary approval within the first month of the lease. The owner collected the $50,000 but the lessee was out the $10,000 lease price plus the $2,500 premium. Furthermore, she had no horse. In this case, the lessor owned a sales barn and allowed the lessee to apply the lease price to another comparable horse or toward the purchase of a horse. More often, the lessor is a private party who owns no other horse, and the lessee is out $12,500 with no horse to ride.

Norma wanted this contract to include a clause providing for a prorated refund to her in the event the lessor collects the mortality insurance, but the lessor, Karen, was unwilling to agree to this term. All contracts are subject to negotiation, and each person tries to get the best deal for himself.

7. The lessor must be relieved of all liability from the acts of the lessee. The gist of this section is that the lessor must be in the same position in terms of potential lawsuits by outsiders as he would if he had sold the horse. If Tax Practice kicks a bystander who sues the owner, Norma must assume any liability. It is as if she owned the horse.

8. The lessor must own the horse. This seems like a redundant paragraph but it protects the lessee, and there have been cases in which agents, unauthorized by the owners, have leased horses.

9. The lessee may request an option to renew the lease, provided the lessor/owner does not choose to sell the horse or use the horse for other purposes.

The lessee may want to tie down the owner in the first year of the lease to the maximum renewal rate. Here they do not set a renewal price. Norma is willing to pay fair market value.

In addition, the right of first refusal is an important clause to the lessee since she has chosen a horse she might like to own.

In this event, the lessee has the right to match an offer from a willing buyer on the open market, and here Norma has protected herself by capping the price at $50,000. The lessor may not agree to this cap if the horse is relatively unproven at the beginning of the lease because, potentially, the horse may be worth more.

10. The lessee must promise to pay the bills. For instance, a problem could arise if the person leasing the horse runs behind on the board bill. In that case, the stable may place a lien on the horse and the true owner cannot retrieve the horse without paying the delinquent barn bill.

11. If either party breaks the agreement on a basic term, then the wronged party collects damages. If the lessee is at fault, the lessor can retrieve the horse. A written notice and warning is strongly advised before either party reverts to self-help. Courts may interpret a material breach quite differently than an owner whose feelings have been hurt.

Finally, the agreement is dated and signed with names, addresses and telephone numbers.

8

Lease – Breeding Services of A Stallion

The lease of a stallion is basically no different in concept from the lease of a school horse or a show horse. One person or persons lease a horse for a set fee for a specific term. The only difference lies in the agreement itself, because the owner and the lessee must include provisions in the contract relevant to stallions and breeding practices.

Example: For tax purposes and because they love horses, the Chenoweths decide to run a small breeding operation. They believe there is a shortage of large athletic thoroughbreds raised in this country for showing and hunting. In response to this perceived need, they have bought large registered mares. They need a quality stallion but the horse they want is out of their price range. However, the owner is willing to lease the stallion to them for a year. They do not own a horse van yet, so they need the horse to be delivered to their farm, and they want the horse for one year to see if the arrangement is successful. They need to make monthly payments because they do not want to deplete their working capital in the first month of the year. They are willing to reserve some breeding rights for the owner of the stallion. They recognize that stallions can be dangerous and plan to buy liability insurance in the event there is an accident caused by the stallion on their property. The Chenoweths are familiar with this stallion, and know he has a high rate of foals. They are anxious to get a signed contract with the owner. The following lease should work for them.

LEASE - BREEDING SERVICES OF STALLION

Lease made ___January 1, 199___ between ___Parkhurst, Inc.___, a corporation organized and existing under the laws of the State of ___New York___, with principal place of business at ___110 Griffin Avenue___, City of ___Riverhead___, County of ___Suffolk___, State of ___New York___, herein referred to as Lessor, and ___Helen Chenoweth___ of ___1035 Jerusalem Road,___, City of ___Kingsville___, County of ___Baltimore___, State of ___Maryland___, herein referred to as Lessee.

Lessor hereby leases to Lessee, who is engaged in the business of breeding horses for the show ring and the hunt field, the below described stallion. In consideration of the terms herein set forth, the parties agree as follows:

1. Description and Delivery of Stallion.

___Lessor___ agrees to deliver Lessor's thoroughbred stallion (''Stallion'') herein described to stand for breeding services at ___Helen Chenoweth's Winter Spring Farm___ at the above described location.

Name	Age	Color	Size	Jockey Club Reg. No.
Cosmic Hill	10	Bay	17 h 2"	J92345

2. Term

The Term of this lease shall be for a period beginning ___January 1, 199___, and ending no later than ___December 31, 199___, or as otherwise provided for herein.

3. Payment

Lessee shall pay a fee of ___Ten Thousand___ dollars ($___10,000.00___) for the stud services of Stallion, payable in ___Four___ (___4___) installments of ___Two Thousand Five Hundred___ dollars ($___2,500.00___). The payment schedule is as follows:

Date	Amount
1/1/9	$2,500.00
4/15/9	$2,500.00
8/15/9	$2,500.00
1/1/9	$2,500.00

Payments not made within ten (10) days of due date will accrue interest on the unpaid balance at 12% per annum.

4. Care and Service by Stallion

(a) Lessee agrees to provide adequate feed, water, shelter, care, maintenance and veterinary care as required in a manner consistent with good thoroughbred practices in the County of __Suffolk__ _____, State of _New York_ at Lessee's expense. This care includes annual vaccinations and regular shoeing and worming. Any specific provisions as to feed, stall size and turnout follow:

(1)

(2)

(b) Lessee covenants that Stallion shall not service in excess of ___Thirty___ (_30_) mares during the breeding season herein described. Lessee will provide a written report of all breedings every sixty (60) days.

(c) Lessor reserves __five__ breeding rights with no fee charged, other than boarding charges on the mares.

5. Uses of Stallion

Lessee covenants not to use the Stallion for any purpose other than breeding as herein provided.

6. Assignment

Lessee shall not assign this lease, or any interest herein, nor sublet Stallion or in any manner permit the use of the Stallion for any purpose other than as herein set forth.

7. Insurance

(a) Lessee shall at his own expense, at all times during term of this lease, maintain in force a policy, written by one or more insurance carriers acceptable to Lessor which shall insure Lessor against liability for injury to or death of persons or damage or loss of property occurring in or about the premises on which the Stallion is used for breeding. The amount of coverage per person, per accident and for property damage must be approved by Lessor. In addition he must receive a copy of said policy within ten days of its effective date.

(b) Lessee agrees to insure Stallion for the lease period with mortality insurance purchased from a company, approved by Lessor, for the sum of $__60,000.00__, said insurance payable to Lessor as beneficiary.

8. Miscellaneous Expenses

Lessee will be responsible to pay all expenses incidental to or consequential of leasing Stallion as if he/she owned Stallion for said term.

9. Permission to Inspect

Lessor may inspect Stallion at any and all times, and Lessee agrees to follow strictly all reasonable instructions, regarding feed, care, handling and breeding of Stallion.

10. Termination of Agreement

(a) At termination for whatever reason, Lessee shall redeliver Stallion to Lessor at above described address at Lessee's expense.

(b) Agreement is terminated on fifteen (15) days written notice if there is a material breach of terms set forth herein.

(c) Any reasonable attorney's fees or court costs incurred as a result of such breach shall be paid by breaching party.

(d) Agreement shall be terminated upon presentation of evidence by a veterinarian that Stallion is unable to successfully impregnate mares for whatever reason. Lessee shall have no right to refund and all payments are still due amd payable in a timely fashion.

11. Lessor's Lien

Lessee grants Lessor a first lien on any foals produced under the terms hereof, under _New York_ law for all unpaid charges on account.

12. Choice of Law

All terms and covenants of this Agreement shall be enforced and constructed in accordance with the laws of the State of _____New York_____.

IN WITNESS WHEREOF, the parties hereto have executed this Lease Agreement as of the day and year above written.

LESSOR: LESSEE:

_____   _____
Signature   Signature

_____
Name of Stallion

_____
Registration Number

Discussion

The Lease begins with an identification of the parties. If the lessor is not a corporation, the person's name or the partnership would be given here. The addresses appear also. Next, the lessee's purpose in leasing the stallion is stated. Here the lessee is planning a breeding operation for show horses and hunters. Often the purpose is to produce race horses.

1. The first terms state who is responsible for delivery of the stallion with a full description of the horse.

2. The term of the lease is set. Here it is for one year.

3. This section states the payment schedule with four installments on a quarterly basis. There is an interest charge for late payments. This gives the Chenoweths a more comfortable financial commitment instead of requiring them to pay a lump sum at the beginning.

4. **(a)** The "Care and Service" terms are set out here. The standard of care language includes the need for annual vaccinations and regular shoeing. The lessor can also add directions for feeding, stall size, and turnout.

   (b) The lease specifies the number of servicings a season with a report due after a two-month period. Here the parties may decide whether the stallion can be used to breed outside mares. If so, the owner may receive a percent of the stud fee.
The owner also reserves a number of breeding rights for his own horses.

5. The stallion may not be used for any purpose not intended by the lessor. If he agrees that the stallion may be shown, raced, or even ridden, this provision must be stated specifically.

6. The lessee cannot sell or give his contract to someone else without the agreement of the lessor. Usually, a right to assignment is limited by the owner's approval, if allowed at all.

7. **(a)** The importance of insurance cannot be underestimated. The owner must protect himself from liability in the event the stallion injures a person or destroys property. He needs assurance from the lessee of adequate coverage and may specify a dollar amount per person and per accident. Insurance companies can advise you here.

   (b) The stallion is also insured for a set amount with the lessor as beneficiary.
The lessee may require a prorated return on the lease fee if the stallion is killed within a certain date. (See discussion on insurance under the Lease form.) The parties may split costs here or determine who pays the premiums.

8. Under "Miscellaneous," the lessee assumes all incidental costs not otherwise listed, such as a new halter, blanket or fly spray.

9. The "Permission to Inspect" is a protection for both parties. The stallion's care must be monitored, and the lessee is responsible for following the lessor's guidelines. The owner should be familiar with the lessee, his stable practices, and his reputation before entrusting the stallion to him. He should be certain the fencing and stabling arrangements are adequate and that a competent professional is handling the breeding operation. He should also not hesitate to exercise his option to inspect the horse during the term of the lease.

10. **(a)** If the Agreement is terminated, the party named (here the lessee) must return the horse to the lessor at the lessee's expense.

   (b) The agreement is ended if one party breaks a material term of the agreement and is notified of this breach in writing.

(c)   The attorney's fees and court costs are paid by the breaching party.

(d)   The agreement is also ended if the stallion is impotent for whatever reason. Here the lessee was familiar with the horse, and could have the horse's fertility analyzed by a veterinarian. The lessee may require a statement of the stallion's past record. Sometimes, the /refund policy is modified for infertility, but the lessors are often unwilling to assume this risk.

11.   The "Lessor's Lien" is a provision giving the lessor a security interest in foals if the lessee doesn't make the payments. This would not be possible, however, if the stallion were breeding mares not owned by the lessee. Otherwise, the lessor could terminate the lease and/or sue for payment.

12.   The "Choice of Law" is applicable in the event of a conflict of state laws, usually if the parties have different state residences or places of business. This is a standard clause in all contracts.

Finally, the contract is executed by signatures. This agreement is a fairly simple version. Several other options may be included:

- The lessor must sign by a certain date all breeding certificates, duly executed for whatever registry is applicable. This clause is to ensure that all offspring are properly registered.
- The live foal guarantees and breedback rights may be specified. In the event of a barren mare or a foal not standing, rebreeding rights are usually provided with the dates specified for the current season or the following year.
- The lessor may reserve an option to lease the horse again for the following year at a set price. Usually, a written notice of this intent is required, and the lessee must inform the lessor of his intent within a certain number of days before the lease in effect expires.

9

Boarding Agreement

When owners keep a horse or horses on someone else's property, they are boarding the horse. A boarding agreement covers the rights and responsibilities of the horse owner and of the stable or farm where the horse is boarded. Board may range from a simple turn out agreement with the owner providing all the food and care to a full service facility.

The need for a formal boarding agreement becomes clear when you consider the following situations.

In one true case, the owner believed she was boarding her pony free in exchange for allowing the pony to be used in the lesson program. The agreement was entirely verbal. After ten months, the parties had widely divergent interpretations of the no-longer-friendly agreement. The stable declared it owned the pony, based on board that was past due. The owner hired a lawyer to regain control of her pony, but, in the meantime, the stable had sold the pony. After a year, the owner received a $500 judgment, but never saw the pony again.

In another instance, an owner loaned his horse to a high school girl who boarded at a nearby stable, but she did not pay her board bills. At the end of the winter, when the owner called to ask for the horse back, he learned he must pay $3,500 in back board or lose his horse to the boarding stable. He did not have $3,500, so he lost his horse.

Example: Maxine, after years of riding lessons, decides to take the big step into horse ownership and buys a horse. She lives in the city, and commutes to the boarding stable where she takes lessons. Her horse, a nonregistered thoroughbred type, costs her $5,000.00. Maxine wants her horse exercised regularly, and, because she cannot be there daily, she needs special services: grooming, blanketing, and tack-up to save her time. She also wants her horse turned out daily, but with only one other horse at a time. Finally, her horse loses weight easily, so needs a specific feeding schedule. Some stables have a standard boarding contract which outlines the responsibilities of the stable and the owner. In this case, Maxine needs to provide her own contract. The following is Maxine's agreement.

SAMPLE

BOARDING AGREEMENT

This Agreement is made _____July 10, 199_____, between _____Oak Cottage Stable_____
_____ (referred to as "Stable") located at _____745 Fireplace Road,_____
East Hampton, New York_____ and Maxine Broke_____ (referred to as
"Owner") residing at _____133 West Barret Street, New York, New York_____,
owner of the horse described in Section 2.

1. Fees

(a) In consideration of $____550.00____ per horse per month paid by Owner in advance on
the first day of each month, the Stable agrees to board said horse beginning ____August 1, 199____
_____.

(b) Options to the basic fee paid in the same timely fashion are available as listed below. Each
additional requested service must be circled and initialed by the owner. These options can be changed
at any time Stable receives written notice from Owner. The fees are subject to change given ____30____
days written notice by Stable.

(1)	Exercise fee	- $ 80.00
(2)	Blanketing when appropriate (owner provides the blanket)	- $ 15.00
(3)	Supplemental vitamins for coat and hoof protein	- $ 15.00
(4)	Daily grooming	- $ 25.00
(5)	Tack-up service with three hours notice	- $ 25.00

2. Description of the Horse(s)

Name: _____Lucky Break_____

Age: _____10 years_____

Color: _____Bay_____

Sex: _____Gelding_____

Breed: _____unknown, t.b. type_____

Height: _____16 hands_____

Registration/Tatoo No.: _____None_____

3. Turn-Out

If no options are chosen, the Owner will be expressly responsible for all exercise and it is
understood that the horse will (will not) be turned out.

4. Standard of Care

All care is provided by Owner.

> **or**

Farm agrees to provide normal and reasonable care to maintain the health and well-being of said horse.

Optional Special Instructions:

(a) Box stall sized 10' by 12'.

(b) Daily turn-out with no more than one other horse.

(c) 10 quarts of sweet feed grain - 10%.

(d) Hay in stall at all times (alfalfa/timothy mix).

5. Risk of Loss

While this horse is boarded at Stable, Stable shall not be liable for any sickness, disease, theft, death or injury suffered by the horse(s) or any other cause of action arising from or connecting to the boarding of this horse. All risks are assumed by the Owner. The Owner agrees to hold Stable harmless from any loss or injury to said horse(s). All costs, no matter how catastrophic, connected with boarding are borne by Owner.

6. Indemnity

Owner agrees to hold Stable harmless from any claim caused by said horse(s) and agrees to pay legal fees incurred by Stable in defense of a claim resulting from damage by said horse(s).

7. Emergency Care

If medical treatment is needed, Stable will attempt calling Owner but, in the event Owner is not reached, Stable has the authority to secure emergency veterinary and/or blacksmith care. Owner is responsible to pay all costs relating to this care. Stable is authorized as Owner's agent to arrange billing to the Owner.

8. Shoeing and Worming

Stable agrees to implement a shoeing and worming program, consistent with recognized standards. Owner is obligated to pay the expenses of such services, including a reasonable stable charge. Such bill shall be paid within fifteen days from the date the bill is submitted to Owner.

9. Ownership - Coggins Test

Owner warrants that he owns the horse and will provide, prior to the time of delivery, proof of a negative Coggins test.

10. Termination

Either party may terminate this agreement. In the event of a default, the wronged party has the right to recover attorneys' fees and court costs, resulting from this failure of either party to meet a material term of this agreement.

11. Notice

Owner agrees to give Stable thirty (30) days notice to terminate this agreement. The Owner cannot assign this agreement unless the Stable agrees in writing.

12. Right of Lien

Stable has the right of lien as set forth in the law of the State of ___New York___ for the amount due for board and additional agreed upon services and shall have the right, without process of law, to retain said horse(s) until the indebtedness is satisfactorily paid in full.

This agreement is subject to the laws of the State of ___New York___.
The parties have executed this agreement this _____ day of
_____, 19_____.

STABLE:
Signed by: _____

                 _____
                 Address
                 _____
                 Telephone

OWNER:
Signed by: _____

                 _____
                 Address
                 _____
                 Telephone

Discussion

In the opening statement, the agreement is dated and the parties are identified. If the stable is incorporated, its title will be followed by "Inc., a corporation of the State of _____ with its principal located _____." The form also provides additional blank space to include the corporate wording where applicable.

1. (a) The basic fee is stated, indicating the monthly board and the due date for accounts receivable. Sometimes the owner receives a reduced rate in exchange for sharing the horse with the stable for lessons. This modified rate can be clarified here. The date the board actually begins is important because the horse's arrival often does not coincide with the date on the contract. Maxine may have signed the agreement on one day, but may not have her horse delivered for two more weeks.

   (b) Overhead in the horse business is very high. Few people recognize the true costs involved in feeding and caring for horses with rising costs for grain, hay, and bedding in a labor-intense business. Stables are advised to collect whatever fees (basic board and additional services) possible at the beginning of each month before the horse moves in. Otherwise, the stable is carrying the boarder for thirty days on its own credit.

Too often, owners are not clear on the services provided and are angry if they think they are not getting their money's worth. This section, stating the extra services and fees saves much bitterness several months after the board has actually begun.

Here the stable describes precisely its additional services and fees. These have been left blank on the sample form and may remain blank if none of these services is provided, or they may be listed with no charge following each item to indicate they are automatically included in the board. In addition, a general supplies charge may be added here to cover the fly spray and saddle soap that is often treated as community property anyway. This charge may also include a laundry fee for pads and bandages.

2. The horse or horses boarded by the owner are described.

3. The turn-out policy is best stated separately. Some stables provide turn-out only and the owner assumes all care of the horse. With the price of land skyrocketing in certain prime locations within commuting distance of large urban areas, it is not uncommon to find a relatively large stable on a small piece of property. Horses may be turnedout in large groups or individually for short periods. This policy needs to be clearly established.

4. All care may be provided by the owner, often called rough board, and the boarding rate is greatly reduced, or, at the other end of the scale, the owner may clarify instruction as to quantity and quality of feed. The stable may specify what the horse will be fed under the boarding fee as stated and may collect additional fees for extras like bedding.

The owner should be familiar with the care provided by the chosen stable and be certain that it is adequate. If he is not experienced in determining this, a professional should be asked to advise.

On the other hand, stables should be aware that owners who insist on feed and schedules not consistent with barn routine and practices may create havoc in a stable feed room. Nevertheless, most stables welcome requests that assist them in maintaining the new boarder's health. (See Stable Record form for in-coming boarders.)

5. This section is imperative because of the high price of stable insurance these days. Some stables require all boarders to be insured, but at very least, liability for loss of the horse must be clearly placed on the owner's shoulders, barring clear malfeasance of the stable or its employees.

6. If the owner's horse injures someone and that person sues the stable, the owner will indemnify (repay) the stable for its costs defending the claim.

7. This clause is meant to protect the horse. For example, if the horse falls and rips open his knee on a stone while the owner is on vacation, the stable is authorized to call the vet to administer emergency care and have the owner billed directly.

The owner, however, should leave a copy of the horse's insurance policy with the stable manager if the policy dictates that a particular procedure be followed before any surgical process is undertaken. The name and number of a preferred vet should also be available to the stable. Stables are advised to contact the owner before deciding on any optional care beyond the immediate need for saving the horse's life.

8. This is the policy for shoeing and worming. Generally, all worming is done at the same time in a barn and both services are most efficiently handled in the barn.

The stables, however, should avoid fronting costs on these services. Direct billing is preferable or the stable can invoke a service charge included for the time and effort.

9. The owner, Maxine, warrants she owns the horse and she must show proof of a negative Coggins test. The Coggins test is widely used to test for a dangerous, usually fatal, contagious disease. This ownership requirement eliminates the situation where the person boarding the horse may not own it, and fails to pay the boarding bill. As noted, the real owner may be liable for the cost of board and may lose his horse to the stable if he cannot afford to pay.

10. This allows the stable or the owner to break the agreement and recover the costs of damages if one side does not abide by the contract. The owner has paid in advance, and he is entitled to have a percent of his fee returned if he must move his horse because the care of the horse is not as agreed. If he must hire a lawyer to collect, he can sue the stable for reasonable costs. Nevertheless, as in all contracts, the parties should try to mediate, because these court cases can be difficult and time consuming to resolve.

11. The owner is required to give the stable thirty days notice before ending the agreement. For instance, a stable usually orders feed and hires help according to its bookings. One horse leaving a stable is usually not a problem, but some owners may own a significant number of horses and it would disrupt a stable if they all left at once. In addition, the stable may have a waiting list and needs time to notify new boarders.

12. This clause provides security for the stable that bills will be paid. The owner may not move the horse until the bill is paid and, under extreme circumstances with written notice, the stable could sell the horse or take over ownership to recoup the unpaid bill.

Different states have different laws and some stables have several locations. The agreement is subject to the laws of the state named in the agreement. The date the agreement is signed appears next with the stable signature by an authorized agent and the owner's signature, with respective addresses and telephones.

10

Training Agreement

A training agreement is a contract between a trainer and a horse owner. The trainer is paid for schooling a horse over a specified period, and the training agreement may include boarding the horse at the trainer's stable. In this case, the cost of the board and the training fees are itemized separately.

Training agreements can become complicated and require written contracts. For instance, when an owner sponsors a trainer, the trainer may receive part ownership of a horse in exchange for publicizing the owner's stable. In one case, a rider contended she was asked by the stable owner to train at his stable for one year in return for part ownership of a horse, yet to be purchased, within a certain price range. They agreed with a handshake that the rider would train and show horses to promote the farm and attract boarders. Later, the owner alleged he had only promised a ten percent ownership in the horse per year as an incentive. In the interim, the horse was purchased and the horse's value increased dramatically. Each party believed he owned the horse. The original contract terms had been verbal and were in complete dispute. After failed mediation, the case landed in court, and the three-week trial ended in a decision in favor of the trainer. The court ruled that the trainer owned the horse under the agreement and the stable owner would receive compensation for the six months the trainer had left to fulfill the contract.

Example: Owner Linda Barnes purchases a green horse, Sky Pilot, to be trained by Nancy Banfield. Linda wants her horse schooled and shown. Eventually, she hopes to show the horse as an adult hunter the following season. Linda has several concerns about the training agreement. She has heard stories of training bills with other trainers that have become excessive, and worries that there will be many unforeseen extra expenses attached to the monthly bills. She also wonders whether she should carry liability or mortalilty insurance.

Furthermore, Linda feels she should get a reduction in the training fee if the horse is lame or injured over an extended period. She also needs a clause relating to the winning of prize money, and finally she does not want to be committed to a long-term agreement. The following contract should suit her.

TRAINING AGREEMENT

THIS TRAINING AGREEMENT (the "Agreement") made this _____ day of _____ 19_____, by and between: _____Linda Barnes_____, hereinafter referred to as "Owner", and _____Nancy Banfield_____ and _____Oak Cottage Stable_____, hereinafter referred to as "Trainer".

WITNESSETH that Owner owns the below described horse(s) and covenants with Trainer to train said horse(s) for the purpose and under the terms hereto agreed as follows:

1. Description of Horse and Delivery

Trainer agrees to arrange transportation to _____Oak Cottage Stable_____ on or about _____July 7_____ at Owner's expense the following described horse(s):

	Name	Age	Color	Sex	Breed
1.	Sky Pilot	5	ch.	gelding	16h.
2.					
3.					
4.					

2. Terms of Payment

Owner shall pay a fee of _____Forty_____ Dollars ($___40.00_____) per day per horse, payable as follows:

(a) Each payment to be due and payable by the first of each month.

(b) Any payment not received by the seventh of each month shall incur interest at 12% per annum for the number of days past the first.

(c) Payment not received by the fifteenth of each month is subject to a $15.00 penalty charge over and above the monthly bill.

3. Additional Expenses

Owner shall be responsible for all costs directly related to this agreement, including but not limited to transportation, veterinary bills, entries, grooming fees and necessary special equipment. Owner will not be responsible for additional expenses exceeding ___One Thousand____ Dollars ($__1,000.00____) per month without prior written approval. All additional expenses are due and payable on the first of the month as provided by Section 2.

4. Trainer Responsibilities

(a) Trainer shall fulfill the duties in a manner consistent with good show training practices in this County of _____ in the State of _____:

1. to maintain the health and well-being of the horse(s) at a level of fitness necessary for light showing.

2. to school the horse on the flat and over fences to the point at which the horse can perform a three (3) foot hunter course at a show with flying changes.

(b) Trainer shall pay all expenses according to Section 2, sending Owner an accounting each month.

In the event Trainer is not reimbursed on time, Trainer is authorized to deduct said payments from any other source available to Trainer.

(c) Trainer shall obtain all necessary veterinary and farrier services and as agent may authorize direct billing. Any extraordinary care over and beyond normal and regular maintenance requires prior written approval by Owner unless involving the most immediate emergency treatment.

5. Showing

(a) Any Prize money won by Owner's horse while under this agreement shall be treated as follows:

1. Trainer receives 50% of said prize money as a bonus.

2. The remaining 50% of said prize money shall be credited to Owner's account.

(b) Owner's horse(s) shall be shown in name of _____ Sky Pilot _____ with Linda Barnes _____ as Owner and _ Nancy Banfield _____ as Trainer.

6. Lay-ups

If said horse(s) is out of training for over _ seven _ days consecutively, Owner shall pay the cost of board at _____ Thirty _____ Dollars ($_ 30.00 _) per day plus incidental expenses as required. Owner must be notified within _ five _ (_ 5 _) days if horse is taken out of training.

7. Term and Termination

(a) The term of this Agreement shall be _____ on a month to month _____ basis. Either party may terminate Agreement given _____ three _____ (_ 3 _) days written notice, provided a final accounting by the Trainer is presented and all payments have been made by Owner prior to taking possession of said horse(s).

(b) On termination, Trainer shall have a lien on said horse(s) under _ Maryland _ law for all unpaid charges on account. Payment must be made in full before said horse(s) is released unless Trainer consents in writing.

8. Insurance

(a) Owner shall bear all risk of loss from the death of or any harm to said horse(s) unless such loss is caused by gross negligence of Trainer; his agents, or employees, in which case Trainer shall bear such loss.

(b) Trainer agrees/does not agree to carry insurance protecting Owner against any losses caused by negligence of Trainer, his agents and employees.

(c) Owner agrees to reimburse Trainer _____% of the premium for said insurance.

(d) Trainer agrees/does not agree to maintain liability insurance.

1. $_____ per person
2. $_____ per accident
3. $_____ property damage

If insurance is so provided, Trainer will make a copy of the policy available to Owner.

9. Indemnification

Owner agrees to indemnify Trainer unless otherwise provided by insurance against all liability or claims, demands, and costs for or arising out of this agreement unless such are caused by the gross negligence of Trainer, his agent or employees.

10. Binding Effect

(a) The parties hereto agree that this Agreement shall be binding on their respective heirs, successors and assigns.

(b) Failure of either party to abide by and perform any and all other terms, covenants, conditions, and obligations of this Agreement shall constitute a default and shall, in addition to any other remedies provided by law or in equity, entitle the wronged party to reasonable attorney fees and court costs related to such breach.

(c) In all respects, this Agreement shall be construed in accordance with, and governed by the laws of _____Maryland_____.

(d) This Agreement contains the final and entire agreement between parties and neither they nor their agents shall be bound by any terms, conditions, or representatives unless amended to this Agreement and initialed by both parties hereto.

IN WITNESS WHEREOF, the parties have executed this Agreement on the day and year first above written.

OWNER: TRAINER:

_____   _____
Signature   Signature

_____   _____
Address   Address

_____   _____

_____   _____
Telephone   Telephone

Discussion

First, the training agreement sets the date of the agreement and names the owner, stable, and trainer. The general purpose is stated, and it is established that the owner owns the horse and desires the trainer to school the horse, and the trainer has consented.

1. The trainer arranges the delivery of the horse at the expense of the owner. The horse or horses are described and the terms of payment are clarified on a per diem cost basis.

2. Bills are due on the first of the month and late payments are subject to an interest charge, set by the parties to the contract. If payment is not received by the fifteenth of each month, there is an additional $15.00 handling fee. These figures are arbitrary, but should not be usurious. Nevertheless, stringent rules are needed to encourage timely payment because of the high overhead of the business.

3. The owner is responsible for all additional expenses, including veterinary charges, show-related costs, and the purchase of training equipment. If the incidental costs exceed a specific amount, prior approval is required. Costs mount quickly and this clause enables the owner to control additional expenses. On the other hand, the trainer may have paid for some charges out of pocket and needs to be assured of reimbursement.

4. The trainer's duties are clarified. The basic standard of care is described, followed by any specific responsibilities.

    (a) The owner should know the trainer and personally examine his operation before entrusting the horse to him. Professional advice is helpful and references provide added reassurance. For instance, the owner should determine if the trainer's horses are healthy and happy looking and are consistent winners. This contract states the owner's expectations in terms of the schooling and showing level.

    (b) The trainer must send a monthly accounting of expenses and is authorized to deduct any unpaid balance from the owner's account.

    (c) The trainer organizes the regular maintenance of vaccinations, worming, shoeing and other medical requirements. He is authorized to arrange direct billing. Any medical expenses over and beyond the customary regular maintenance require prior approval unless they involve emergency treatment.

5. The allocation of prize money is optional. Some Owners keep 100% of the money, but usually the trainer and owner split the prize money. This section also clarifies the horse's show name and the ownership for show purposes. This prevents a trainer from showing a client's horse under his own name.

6. Linda was concerned that her horse might go lame or be taken out of training for some other purpose. Under the terms of this section, she will be notified when her horse is not in work and charged a reduced rate.

7. The term of this Agreement can be any length. Here it is on a month-to-month basis, as Linda prefers. A contract like this is rarely more than a year with the ability to renew. Either side may end the agreement with three days' written notice, but the owner cannot take the horse off the premises without settling the bill. The trainer has a lien on the horse under state law and can, under the worst case scenario, sell the horse at auction to settle the account. For this reason, trainers are advised to keep accounts current; there can be times when the horse is not worth the bill, and the owner is broke.

8. Insurance is optional, but recommended, because it protects all parties, especially the owner who must bear the loss if the horse is injured or dies.

In addition, this clause releases the trainer and his agents from all liability unless there is gross negligence. Many contracts release them from all liability, including any level of negligence. This is a negotiable point. Trainers are well advised to carry liability insurance in the event a horse injures someone on their property, and the owner will often require this safeguard and be willing to pay a part of the premium.

9. In the event there is no insurance or a claim exceeds the insurance, the owner will reimburse the trainer for any claims relating to the owner's horse.

10. (a) The agreement binds all succeeding parties in case the original person dies or a subsequent person is assigned in his place, for example, if a parent assigns ownership of the horse to a relative.

(b) The person who breaks the terms of the agreement will be responsible for all reasonable legal fees if an attorney or court costs are involved.

(c) The laws of one resident state are chosen to govern.

(d) Too often the parties start altering the terms of a contract verbally and this leads to confusion and often conflict later. Any alterations in the agreement must be added in writing.

Finally, both parties execute the agreement by signing it.

11

Release and Hold Harmless Agreement

A release and hold harmless agreement is a release signed by an adult for himself or as a parent or guardian stating that he is aware of the risks in riding and working around horses and will not sue the stable for damages in the event of an accident to himself or his child.

Example: Pam is opening a stable that will employ several instructors, but remembers that a friend of hers was forced into bankruptcy through a lawsuit by a client who was injured on a trail ride. Pam plans to buy liability insurance but would like all students and boarders at her stable, Winter Springs Farm, to sign a release form. Pam wants a form that is inclusive (see General Discussion) and will make it clear to her clients that they assume the risks fully and will not hold her responsible for any direct or related injuries. She borrows a form used by a local stable, Leaky Roof.

I, _____Robert_____, assume responsibility for _myself_____ to ride horseback at _____Leaky Roof Stable_____. I understand that neither _____Leaky Roof Stable_____ nor its employees will be held responsible for accidents, illnesses or injury connected with the ___Leaky Roof Stable_____ Riding Program.

_____
_____

Date __4/2/92__   Name_Robert Wright_____
                         Address_9220 Valley Road_____
                         Phone_(301) 882-7560_____

SAMPLE

RELEASE AND HOLD HARMLESS AGREEMENT

The Undersigned assumes the unavoidable risks inherent in all horse-related activities, including but not limited to bodily injury and physical harm to horse, rider, and spectator.

In consideration, therefore, for the privilege of riding and/or working around horses at Winter Springs Farm , located at Evna Road, Parkton, Maryland , the Undersigned does hereby agree to hold harmless and indemnify Winter Springs Farm and further release them from any liability or responsibility for accident, damage, injury, or illness to the Undersigned or to any horse owned by the Undersigned or to any family member or spectator accompanying the Undersigned on the premises.

_____
Signature

_____
Print Name, Address, and Telephone Number

_____

_____

_____
Signature of Parent or Guardian

General Discussion

Release forms are a must for all formal and informal riding programs, but they should not in any way lull the business owner into thinking he/she does not need liability insurance. Lawsuits arise with and without releases.

Parents must sign the form or they will have no binding value because minors cannot sign binding contracts. By signing the release the parents or guardian cannot assume the minor's risk. In other words, lawsuits are not avoidable. Visitors may sue the stable and indemnification clauses are not a protective veil. Courts look at factors of negligence and the standard of care.

The grounds for losing lawsuits are many, but most are the result of unsafe conditions established by the stable, in spite of releases. Stables have been forced into bankruptcy for creating risks over and beyond what the client has willingly assumed. In a recent case, a stable was successfully sued for sending a client out on what the court deemed was an unsuitable horse.

To prevent these situations from arising, it is recommended that stables establish the following rules:

(1) All riders must be required to wear protective headgear.

(2) Equipment must be inspected and kept in good repair.

(3) Horses with records of unsafe practices should be removed from the riding program.

(4) Instruction must be competent and instructors well-qualified. This country does not license riding teachers, so the stable needs at least a resume on its teachers with documented proof of their competency.

(5) Close supervision of all horse-related activities is essential.

Most insurance companies require releases as a condition of a policy and may reduce the premiums if written personal and boarding releases are required.

Discussion of Release and Hold Harmless Agreement

The person who signs the agreement (not a minor) assumes the risks inherent in all horse-related activities. For the privilege of riding at the particular stable, this person agrees the stable owner or any employees will not be liable for any damages and will pay the stable owner for any expense incurred as a result of a liability arising from an injury to a family member or guest of the undersigned.

The release will not protect against "malpractice." If a stable does not follow safety procedures or takes unreasonable risks, no release will shield the owner/instructor and/or employees from liability.

12

Stable Record

The stable record is a bookkeeping form to document the dates of farrier visits and veterinarian care. All vaccinations and wormings are recorded along with any special instructions.

The following form is not a legal form but it relates to the standard of care under the boarding contract. This form improves stable efficiency and protects the stable if the standard of care is in question. For the owner, it ensures up-to-date, timely care. These forms can be entered in a loose-leaf notebook for simple record keeping and can be presented to the stable each time a horse moves. Each horse needs a record of care for vetting and shoeing purposes.

The front page covers worming, tubing, vaccinations, Coggins tests and dental care. It can be modified based on the practices of the area and the veterinarian's recommendations. The back of the sheet includes a shoeing schedule with records of injury and treatment.

STABLE RECORD

Horse _____''Field'' (Field Audit)_____ Birth Date _____6/7/84_____
Description _____Chestnut Gelding_____ Height _____16 h 3"_____
Acquired from _____J. Moyland_____ Date _____1/8/90_____
General Info: _____Do not turn out with bells or boots; wrap hind legs_____
_____after hard work-out._____

	199			
Worming 4 x /year	Feb/Iver.			
Tubed	4/19/9 strongid			
Flu Vaccine 2 x /year	4/19/9			
Eastern/Western 1 x per yr.	4/19/9			
Tetanus 1 x per yr.	4/19/9			
PHF	4/19/9			
Rabies 1 x per yr.	4/19/9			
Rhinomune	4/19/9			
Coggins 1 x per yr.	4/19/9 neg 5/8			
Teeth floated 1 x per yr.	4/19/9			
Other:	(Dr. Tanner)			

Date	Shoeing	Injury or Sickness/Treatment
4/25	2 hind/clips $38	6/30 Sprained hock, 10 days rest with bute

Glossary

The following is a list of financial and legal terms used in this book with their definitions. Note that the definitions are limited to the specialized uses of these terms in the context of this volume.

Aggregate Dollar Amount: The total amount, including interest or additional related costs.

Amortization Schedule: A reduction in a debt by periodic payments covering interest and part of principal.

Assigns: Persons who are given an interest or full ownership in a property by the owner usually through a will, trust, or as a gift.

Capital: Investment money, the amount invested in a business.

Consideration: Any payment received in the form of money, property, or services.

Covenant: To promise or to agree to something as in a contract.

Encumbrance: Any interest in property that might interfere with the sale of the property, as in a claim, lein, charge, or liability attached to and binding real property.

Hypothecate: To offer something as security as in to mortgage property.

Investment Security: Any corporate bonds or corporate obligation secured by property owned by the corporation; a written obligation giving the holder the right to receive property not in his possession.

Legatee: A person who receives property under a will.

Lien: A charge against or interest in property to secure payment of a debt or performance of an obligation.

Net Cash: The amount of money left over after all the bills have been paid.

Notice: The letter informing a person of a change in a contract or a problem concerning a contract or the date of a meeting.

Par Value: A dollar amount assigned to a share by the company.

Partnership Information Form (Form 1065):   An annual information return stating all items of income and deductions. Also included are the names and addresses of all partners and the amount of each partner's distributive share that year.

Passive Activity: Businesses in which a person does not materially participate based on tests of hours spent. The IRS has devised seven tests to determine material participation. Some tests require only a minimum amount of work, in some cases just more than 100 hours annually.

Passive Activity Loss Limitations: Rules that limit the deduction of losses from a passive activity to offset income from other passive activities. The following are not considered passive income: salary, self-employment earnings from a regular job, interest, dividends, royalties, retirement income, or gains from the sale of stock or similar investment property.

Passive Activities: Include rental operations, income as a limited partner, and all businesses in which the person does not materially participate.

Profit/Loss: The difference between the cost of the horse and the amount you receive for the horse.

Pursuant: In agreement with or in accordance with.

Testamentary Disposition: Something received through a will or a trust at someone's death.

Title: The right to ownership, also the evidence of ownership.

Waiver (n.):   A voluntary, intentional relinquishment of a known right.

Appendix:
Blank Forms

LIST OF FORMS

SYNDICATE

AGREEMENT, made _____ between the persons whose names and addresses are set out in the Schedule attached and who have subscribed for the number of units set forth opposite their names (''Owners'').

RECITALS

The Owners desire to form a Syndicate to purchase the _____,

_____

herein referred to as the ''horse''.

The Owners will pay the sum of $ _____ per unit. There shall be _____ units in this Syndicate. _____, acting for this Syndicate shall purchase the horse for the sum of $ _____ and will accept delivery of the horse.

Upon said purchase of the horse, the Syndicate shall be in existence for the ownership and management of the horse upon the following terms and conditions:

1. Ownership.

The ownership of the horse shall be _____ units, to be insured at a price of $ _____ per unit; each of the _____ units be on an equal basis with the others, and only a full unit shall have any rights.

2. Location.

The horse shall be stabled at _____

_____,

_____

subject to change by consensus, and shall be under the personal supervision of _____ _____, as Syndicate Manager.

3. Manager's Duties.

Subject to the approval of the Partner(s), the Syndicate Manager shall have full charge of and control over the management of the horse and of all training matters arising out of this enterprise, subject to the approval of the Owners.

She shall keep accurate account of all show records. She shall exercise her best judgment in all training decisions.

4. Transferability.

Units may be transferred subject to the terms of this agreement; provided, however, that each Owner shall have the first refusal to purchase any unit or units which an Owner may desire to sell.

5. Expenses.

Each Owner shall pay his proper share of the expenses of the Syndicate, including organizational, legal, accounting, board, advertising, veterinary, etc., proportionate to the number of units which he holds. Bills will be sent out monthly and are payable within ten days.

6. Liability of Manager.

The Syndicate Manager shall not be personally liable for any act or omission committed by her except for willful misconduct or gross negligence.

7. Insurance.

The Syndicate Manager shall be responsible for insuring the horse. The expense of the insurance shall be shared by the Partners in accordance with this agreement.

8. Accounting.

The Syndicate Manager shall furnish each Partner periodically with a statement showing the receipts and expenditures and such other information as she may deem pertinent.

9. Special Meetings.

A special meeting of the Partner(s) may be called by either Partner at any time of mutual convenience with reasonable notice.

10. Active Participation.

Notwithstanding Manager's duties, each Partner shall materially and substantially participate in the day-to-day decisions affecting and relating to this joint venture and all management decisions relating to said horse.

11. Notices.

All required notices shall be effective and binding if sent by prepaid registered mail, telegram, cable, or delivered in person to the address of the respective Owners set out in the Schedule attached. Such address changes shall hereafter be designated in writing to the Syndicate Manager, addressed to:_____

_____

_____.

12. Miscellaneous.

This Agreement, when executed by the Owners, shall constitute the agreement between the parties, and shall be binding upon the Owners, their heirs, and assigns.

13. Liability.

This Agreement shall not be deemed to create any relationship by reason of which any party might be held liable for the omission or commission of any other party, unless otherwide provided.

14. Termination.

This Syndicate terminates on the sale of the horse at which time the Syndicate Manager shall furnish each Partner with an accounting. All income and expenses shall be shared in accordance with the proportionate ownership of units.

IN WITNESS WHEREOF we have executed this Agreement the day and date first above written.

_____
Signature

_____
Address

_____
Units Purchased

_____
Signature

_____
Address

_____
Units Purchased

BILL OF SALE

I, _____, residing at _____
_____ in consideration of _____
_____, hereby paid to me by _____,
residing at _____, sell to
_____ the following described horse:

Name: _____

Age: _____

Color: _____

Breed: _____

Sex: _____

Size: _____

    I hereby covenant that I am the lawful owner of the horse; that I have the right to sell the horse; and that I will warrant and defend said horse against lawful claims and demands of all persons.
    Executed this _____ day of _____, 19 _____.

_____

Signature of Seller

CONSIGNMENT AGREEMENT

THIS AGREEMENT is made between _____, the "Consignor", residing at _____, and _____, the "Consignee", residing at _____.

1. Description

The Consignor owns a horse described in this section below:

(a) Name: _____

(b) Age: _____

(c) Breed: _____

(d) Sex: _____

(e) Size: _____

2. Purpose

The Consignor is in the business of buying and selling horses as an agent. The Consignor desires to sell said horse. Consignee agrees to make his best effort to sell said horse on behalf of the Consignor.

3. Warranties

The Consignee accepts said horse into his sales barn under the following terms:

(a) _____
_____
_____

(b) _____
_____
_____

(c) _____
_____
_____

(d) _____
_____
_____

4. Board

In consideration of _____ per horse per month paid by Consignor in advance on the first day of each month, the Consignee agrees to board said horse until sold or this Agreement is terminated.

5. Commission

At the sale of said horse, the Consignee shall receive a commission of _____% on all funds received. The Consignor shall receive the balance of all funds on the sale of said horse within 10 days. The Consignee shall charge _____% late fee per month on any late payment.

6. Care of Horse

(a) The Consignee agrees to provide normal and reasonable care to maintain the health and well-being of said horse. This care includes (i) _____,
(ii) _____, and (iii) _____
_____,

(b) Routine veterinary and farrier care are authorized with direct billing. Any extraordinary care requires the consent of the Consignor unless on an emergency basis.

(c) The following feed and supplements shall be fed daily:

Hay: _____ _____

Grain: _____ _____

Daily supplements:

_____

_____

_____

(d) Exercise

Said horse shall be ridden or lunged by Consignee or a competent rider employed by Consignee at least _____ days a week.

The Consignee will show the horse to potential buyers under the following terms.

(1)_____

_____

(2)_____

_____

(3)_____

_____

7. Assumption of Risk at Sale

The Buyer takes possession only upon transfer of full consideration to Consignee. The risk of loss passes to Buyer at the Consignee's farm upon delivery of any relevant registration papers and a bill of sale. Buyer assumes all costs at the point of said transfer and prior to the horse's release from Consignee's premises.

None of the above terms are subject to change without explicit written agreement by the Consignor.

8. Lien

Consignee agrees to keep horse free and clear of all liens and encumbrances.

9. Attorney's Fees

This Agreement is terminated upon a breach of any material term and the wronged party has the right to collect all reasonable fees and costs from the breaching party.

10. Termination

Either party may cancel this agreement prior to sale on _____ days written notice and final accounting thereto.

11. Governing Law

In all respects, this Agreement shall be constructed in accordance with and governed by the laws of the State of _____.

_____   _____
Dated   Signature of Consignor

_____   _____
Dated   Signature of Consignee

LIMITED POWER OF ATTORNEY

I, _____, of _____,

do hereby execute this Limited Power of Authority with the intention that the attorney-in-fact hereinaf-

ter named shall be able to act in my place for the purposes set forth herein.

SECTION 1. Designation of Attorney.

I constitute and appoint _____

_____ to be my

attorney-in-fact to act for me, in my name, and in

my place.

SECTION 2. Effective Date of Power of Attorney.

2.01 This Limited Power of Attorney shall be effective as of the date of its execution by me, and shall remain effective unless same revoked by me, until midnight on _____.

2.02 This Limited Power of Attorney shall not be affected by my disability, it being my specific intention that my attorney-in-fact shall continue to act as such even though I may not be competent to ratify the actions of my attorney-in-fact.

SECTION 3. Powers.

3.01 My attorney-in-fact shall have all of the powers, discretions, elections, and authorities granted by statute, common law, and under any rule of court necessary to sell my _____

_____

_____

_____.

In addition thereto, and not in limitation thereof, my attorney-in-fact shall also have the power set forth below.

3.02 My attorney-in-fact may collect and receive, with or without the institution of suit or other legal process, all debts, monies, objects,

interest, and demands due to me pursuant to the aforementioned sale.

3.03 My attorney-in-fact may endorse my name for deposit into a savings, checking, or money-market account of mine with respect to sums payable to me pursuant to the aforementioned sale.

3.04 My attorney-in-fact may execute, seal, acknowledge, and deliver any documents necessary, advisable or expedient with respect to the aforementioned sale.

SECTION 4. Ratification.

4.01 I hereby ratify, allow, acknowledge, and hold firm and valid all acts heretofore or hereafter taken by my attorney-in-fact by virtue of these presents in connection with the afore-mentioned contract.

AS WITNESS my hand and seal this _____ day of _____, 19_____.

WITNESS:

_____

_____

(SEAL)

BILL OF SALE
WITH PROMISSORY NOTE

THIS BILL OF SALE, made this _____, day of _____, by and between _____, hereinafter called Seller, and _____ _____ hereinafter called Buyer.

    1. That in consideration of the payment of _____, _____ in cash and a _____ promissory note, by the Buyer to the Seller, the receipt of which is hereby acknowledged, said Seller does hereby bargain, sell, transfer, assign and convey unto said Buyer, its successors and assigns, free and clear of all debts, liens and encumbrances, the horse as described below:

    A. Name: _____

    B. Age: _____

    C. Color: _____

    D. Breed: _____

    E. Sex: _____

    F. Size: _____

    2. The Seller hereby represents that said horse hereby sold is his/her horse and that title is vested and that it has a good and perfect right to sell same, and that no debts, claims, obligations or encumbrances exist on or against said horse.

    WITNESS, the hands of the Seller and Buyer.

WITNESS:

_____   _____

                                   _____
                                   Address

                                   _____
                                   Telephone

                                   _____
                                   Address

                                   _____
                                   Telephone

PROMISSORY NOTE

THIS AGREEMENT is made between _____

(the "Undersigned") and _____.

1. Consideration

FOR VALUE RECEIVED, _____
_____ does hereby
promise to pay to the order of _____
_____ the sum of _____
_____ Dollars ($_____),
together with interest on the unpaid principal
balance at the rate of _____ Percent
(_____%) per annum from the date hereof
in installments beginning on _____
_____ and on the first of each month
thereafter in the amount of $_____
until the entire principal balance is paid in full or
until _____ thereafter, at
which time the amount then owing shall be due.

2. Payment Terms

The monthly payments are calculated on an
amortization schedule of _____
years and the full amount then owing shall be
due _____ years from the date of the
first payment, unless otherwise accelerated under
the terms and conditions hereof. Both principal
and interest shall be payable at the address of
_____ at
_____
_____, or at such
other address as may be designated from time to
time by written notification to the Undersigned
by the holder hereof.

3. Prepayment

The Undersigned shall have the right to
prepay, at any time or times, without penalty, all
or any part of the balance of the principal hereof.
Any such prepayment shall be applied first to
any unpaid interest accrued hereunder and then
to the principal, in which case the amounts due
with respect to succeeding interest payments
hereunder shall be adjusted accordingly.

4. Default

In the event (any of which events shall be
deemed an "event of default"): (a) the Undersigned shall fail to make any payment of principal or interest when due hereunder and such
failure shall have continued for ten (10) days
after written notice of such default by the holder
hereof, or (b) any voluntary petition by, or
involuntary petition against, the Undersigned
shall be filed under any chapter of the Federal
Bankruptcy Act, or any proceeding involving the
Undersigned shall be instituted under any other
law relating to the relief of debtors, and such
petition or proceeding shall not be vacated within
ten (10) days thereafter, or (c) the Undersigned
shall make any assignment for the benefit of
creditors, or (d) a judgment shall be entered
against the Undersigned in any court of record
and shall not be satisfied within five (5) days
thereafter, then the holder hereof, in his, his/her
or their sole discretion may declare this Promissory Note to be due forthwith, and the same shall
thereupon become immediately due and payable
in full, all without any presentment, demand or
notice of any kind, which are hereby waived.

5. Rights of Holder

No delay or omission on the part of the
holder hereof in the exercise of any right or
remedy shall operate as a waiver thereof, and no
single or partial exercise by the holder of any
right or remedy shall preclude other or further
exercise of any right or remedy.

6. Remedies

The Undersigned hereby authorizes any
attorney of any court within the State of
_____ or elsewhere to confess
judgment against the Undersigned at any time
after this Promissory Note is due (whether upon

normal maturity or acceleration hereunder), hereby waiving all exemptions, for the principal amount of this Promissory Note and interest and attorney's fees and court costs. If this Promissory Note is referred to an attorney for collection, then there shall be added to the amount due and owing hereunder reasonable attorney's fees of not less than 15% or such amount as any Court in which an action is filed deems to be reasonable, plus costs of collection.

7. Waiving of Defenses

The Undersigned hereby waives presentment, demand, notice of dishonor, protest and all other demands and notices whatsoever in connection with the delivery, acceptance, performance and enforcement of this Note.

Executed this _____ day of
_____, 19_____.

_____

_____
Address
_____

_____
Telephone

PURCHASE AGREEMENT

THIS AGREEMENT is made between _____ , residing at
_____ (''Buyer'') and
_____ , residing at _____
_____ (''Seller'') for the purchase described below:

Name: _____

Age: _____

Color: _____

Breed: _____

Sex: _____

Size: _____

1. Purchase Price
For the total sum of $_____ , Seller agrees to sell and Buyer agrees to buy said horse based on the terms to follow.

2. Payment Terms
The Buyer agrees to pay $_____ , as a deposit on _____
_____ and the balance due of $_____ on
_____ .

3. Warranties
   (a) Seller covenants that he/she is the lawful owner of said horse; that he/she has the right to sell said horse; and that he will warrant and defend the horse against lawful claims and demands of all persons.

   (b) Seller makes no other promises, express or implied, including the warranties of fitness for a particular purpose unless further provided in this Agreement.

   (c) Seller warrants the following: _____
_____

   (d) Buyer waives any claim for damage should said horse fail to meet the above warranties at the time of delivery, unless such defect is discovered within _____ days from delivery to Buyer.

4. Transfer of Ownership
Once Seller has received payment in full, Seller shall transfer all owner and registration papers of the horse at his own expense.

5. Risk of Loss
Seller assumes all risk of loss until the Buyer takes delivery or until the Buyer begins transfer of the horse, whichever comes first.

6. Law

The terms of this Agreement shall be governed by the laws of the State of _____.

7. Breach

Either party may nullify this Agreement if the other party breaches a material term of this Agreement. The wronged party may recover reasonable attorney's fees and court costs.

    Executed this _____ day of _____, 19_____.

SELLER: BUYER:

_____   _____
Signature   Signature

_____   _____
Address   Address

LEASE AGREEMENT

This Lease is made _____ between _____

residing at _____, (hereinafter

referred to as "Lessor" and _____, residing on _____

_____, (hereinafter referred to as "Lessee").

1. Term

The term of this Lease shall be for a period beginning _____

and ending no later than _____, or as otherwise provided for

herein:

2. Description

This Lease covers the horse(s) described in this section below.

A. Name: _____

B. Age: _____

C. Breed: _____

D. Sex: _____

E. Size: _____

3. Consideration/Payment

Lessee shall pay a fee of _____,

payable as follows:

Payment   Date

_____   _____

_____   _____

_____   _____

4. Uses of Horse and Limitations

Lessee covenants not to use the horse for any purpose other than as set forth: _____

_____

_____.

Lessor promises that said horse is capable and suited for said purpose. Lessor explicitly denies
the right to any other party for any sublease agreement, barring all other riders except the Lessee's
instructor or chosen professional rider where appropriate.

5. Instructions for Care

Lessee will follow all practices consistent with quality care _____

_____ at Lessee's own expense. Lessee shall provide all necessary
veterinarian and blacksmith needs at Lessee's own expense. In addition said horse requires:

(a) _____

(b) _____

(c) _____

(d) _____

(Grain rations and hay plus stall size can be stated here.)

6. Risk of Loss and Insurance

(a) Lessee assumes risk of loss or injury to said horse(s), barring an act of the Lessor or Lessor's agent.

(b) Lessee shall at his/her own expense at all times during the term of this lease maintain in force a policy or policies of insurance written by one or more responsible insurance carriers acceptable to Lessor. A copy of said policy must be mailed to Lessor within a month of taking delivery.

The liability under such policy shall not be less than _____
_____ payable to the Lessor as sole beneficiary.

7. Hold Harmless

Lessee agrees to hold Lessor harmless from any act of negligence of Lessee or any of his agents, contractors or employees, or arising from any accident, injury, or damage whatsoever however caused to any person or persons, or to the property of any person, persons, or corporations occurring during such term of this Lease and arising out of the use or care of said horse.

8. Ownership

Lessor warrants that he/she owns said horse free and clear and has the right to execute this Lease.

9. Options

(a) Lessee has the option to renew this Lease for an additional _____ (_____) months if a request is made in writing _____ days prior to the expiration of this Lease, provided the horse is available for a lease.

(b) If horse is placed up for sale, the Lessee has the right of first refusal to purchase said horse within _____ (_____) months of the expiration of said lease not to exceed _____
_____.

10. Covenant Not to Encumber

Lessee agrees not to encumber said horse(s) with any lien, charge, or related claim and to hold Lessor harmless therefrom.

11. Default

Upon material breach of this Agreement, Lessor reserves the right to remove such horse without incurring any responsibility to Lessee.

This Agreement is terminated upon a breach of any material term and the other party has the right to collect all reasonable fees and costs from the breaching party.

Signed this _____ day of _____, 19_____.

LESSOR:

_____
Signature

_____
Address

_____
Telephone

LESSEE:

_____
Signature

_____
Address

_____
Telephone

LEASE - BREEDING SERVICES OF STALLION

Lease made _____ between _____, a corporation organized and existing under the laws of the State of _____, with principal place of business at _____, City of _____, County of _____, State of _____, herein referred to as Lessor, and _____ of _____, City of _____, County of _____, State of _____, herein referred to as Lessee.

 Lessor hereby leases to Lessee, who is engaged in the business of breeding horses for the show ring and the hunt field, the below described stallion. In consideration of the terms herein set forth, the parties agree as follows:

1. Description and Delivery of Stallion.
_____ agrees to deliver Lessor's thoroughbred stallion ("Stallion") herein described to stand for breeding services at _____ _____ at the above described location.

Name	Age	Color	Size	Jockey Club Reg. No.

2. Term
 The Term of this lease shall be for a period beginning _____, and ending no later than _____, or as otherwise provided for herein.

3. Payment
 Lessee shall pay a fee of _____ dollars ($_____) for the stud services of Stallion, payable in _____ (_____) installments of _____ _____ dollars ($_____). The payment schedule is as follows:

Date	Amount
_____	_____
_____	_____
_____	_____
_____	_____

  Payments not made within ten (10) days of due date will accrue interest on the unpaid balance at 12% per annum.

4. Care and Service by Stallion
(a) Lessee agrees to provide adequate feed, water, shelter, care, maintenance and veterinary care

as required in a manner consistent with good thoroughbred practices in the County of _____
_____, State of _____ at Lessee's expense. This care includes annual vaccinations and regular shoeing and worming. Any specific provisions as to feed, stall size and turnout follow:

      (1)

      (2)

    (b) Lessee covenants that Stallion shall not service in excess of _____ (_____) mares during the breeding season herein described. Lessee will provide a written report of all breedings every sixty (60) days.

    (c) Lessor reserves _____ breeding rights with no fee charged, other than boarding charges on the mares.

5. Uses of Stallion

Lessee covenants not to use the Stallion for any purpose other than breeding as herein provided.

6. Assignment

Lessee shall not assign this lease, or any interest herein, nor sublet Stallion or in any manner permit the use of the Stallion for any purpose other than as herein set forth.

7. Insurance

    (a) Lessee shall at his own expense, at all times during term of this lease, maintain in force a policy, written by one or more insurance carriers acceptable to Lessor which shall insure Lessor against liability for injury to or death of persons or damage or loss of property occurring in or about the premises on which the Stallion is used for breeding. The amount of coverage per person, per accident and for property damage must be approved by Lessor. In addition he must receive a copy of said policy within ten days of its effective date.

    (b) Lessee agrees to insure Stallion for the lease period with mortality insurance purchased from a company, approved by Lessor, for the sum of $_____, said insurance payable to Lessor as beneficiary.

8. Miscellaneous Expenses

Lessee will be responsible to pay all expenses incidental to or consequential of leasing Stallion as if he/she owned Stallion for said term.

9. Permission to Inspect

Lessor may inspect Stallion at any and all times, and Lessee agrees to follow strictly all reasonable instructions, regarding feed, care, handling and breeding of Stallion.

10. Termination of Agreement

    (a) At termination for whatever reason, Lessee shall redeliver Stallion to Lessor at above described address at Lessee's expense.

    (b) Agreement is terminated on fifteen (15) days written notice if there is a material breach of terms set forth herein.

    (c) Any reasonable attorney's fees or court costs incurred as a result of such breach shall be paid by breaching party.

    (d) Agreement shall be terminated upon presentation of evidence by a veterinarian that Stallion is unable to successfully impregnate mares for whatever reason. Lessee shall have no right to refund and all payments are still due amd payable in a timely fashion.

11. Lessor's Lien

Lessee grants Lessor a first lien on any foals produced under the terms hereof, under _____ law for all unpaid charges on account.

12. Choice of Law

All terms and covenants of this Agreement shall be enforced and constructed in accordance with the laws of the State of _____.

IN WITNESS WHEREOF, the parties hereto have executed this Lease Agreement as of the day and year above written.

LESSOR: LESSEE:

_____   _____
Signature   Signature

_____
Name of Stallion

_____
Registration Number

BOARDING AGREEMENT

This Agreement is made _____, between _____
_____ (referred to as "Stable") located at _____
_____ and _____ (referred to as
"Owner") residing at _____,
owner of the horse described in Section 2.

1. Fees

(a) In consideration of $_____ per horse per month paid by Owner in advance on
the first day of each month, the Stable agrees to board said horse beginning _____
_____.

(b) Options to the basic fee paid in the same timely fashion are available as listed below. Each
additional requested service must be circled and initialed by the owner. These options can be changed
at any time Stable receives written notice from Owner. The fees are subject to change given _____
days written notice by Stable.

(1) _____ - $_____

(2) _____ - $_____

(3) _____ - $_____

(4) _____ - $_____

(5) _____ - $_____

2. Description of the Horse(s)

Name: _____

Age: _____

Color: _____

Sex: _____

Breed: _____

Height: _____

Registration/Tatoo No.: _____

3. Turn-Out

If no options are chosen, the Owner will be expressly responsible for all exercise and it is
understood that the horse will (will not) be turned out.

4. Standard of Care
All care is provided by Owner.

> **or**

Farm agrees to provide normal and reasonable care to maintain the health and well-being of said horse.

Optional Special Instructions:

(a) _____

(b) _____

(c) _____

(d) _____

5. Risk of Loss
While this horse is boarded at Stable, Stable shall not be liable for any sickness, disease, theft, death or injury suffered by the horse(s) or any other cause of action arising from or connecting to the boarding of this horse. All risks are assumed by the Owner. The Owner agrees to hold Stable harmless from any loss or injury to said horse(s). All costs, no matter how catastrophic, connected with boarding are borne by Owner.

6. Indemnity
Owner agrees to hold Stable harmless from any claim caused by said horse(s) and agrees to pay legal fees incurred by Stable in defense of a claim resulting from damage by said horse(s).

7. Emergency Care
If medical treatment is needed, Stable will attempt calling Owner but, in the event Owner is not reached, Stable has the authority to secure emergency veterinary and/or blacksmith care. Owner is responsible to pay all costs relating to this care. Stable is authorized as Owner's agent to arrange billing to the Owner.

8. Shoeing and Worming
Stable agrees to implement a shoeing and worming program, consistent with recognized standards. Owner is obligated to pay the expenses of such services, including a reasonable stable charge. Such bill shall be paid within fifteen days from the date the bill is submitted to Owner.

9. Ownership - Coggins Test
Owner warrants that he owns the horse and will provide, prior to the time of delivery, proof of a negative Coggins test.

10. Termination
Either party may terminate this agreement. In the event of a default, the wronged party has the right to recover attorneys' fees and court costs, resulting from this failure of either party to meet a material term of this agreement.

11. Notice
Owner agrees to give Stable thirty (30) days notice to terminate this agreement. The Owner cannot assign this agreement unless the Stable agrees in writing.

12. Right of Lien
Stable has the right of lien as set forth in the law of the State of _____ for the amount due for board and additional agreed upon services and shall have the right, without process of law, to retain said horse(s) until the indebtedness is satisfactorily paid in full.

This agreement is subject to the laws of the State of _____.

    The parties have executed this agreement this _____ day of _____,
19_____.

STABLE:

Signed by: _____

                   _____

                   Address

                   _____

                   Telephone

OWNER:

Signed by: _____

                   _____

                   Address

                   _____

                   Telephone

TRAINING AGREEMENT

THIS TRAINING AGREEMENT (the "Agreement") made this _____ day of _____ 19_____, by and between: _____, hereinafter referred to as "Owner", and _____ and _____, hereinafter referred to as "Trainer".

    WITNESSETH that Owner owns the below described horse(s) and covenants with Trainer to train said horse(s) for the purpose and under the terms hereto agreed as follows:

1. Description of Horse and Delivery

    Trainer agrees to arrange transportation to _____ on or about _____ at Owner's expense the following described horse(s):

Name	Age	Color	Sex	Breed
1.				
2.				
3.				
4.				

2. Terms of Payment

    Owner shall pay a fee of _____ Dollars ($_____) per day per horse, payable as follows:

    (a) Each payment to be due and payable by the first of each month.

    (b) Any payment not received by the seventh of each month shall incur interest at 12% per annum for the number of days past the first.

    (c) Payment not received by the fifteenth of each month is subject to a $15.00 penalty charge over and above the monthly bill.

3. Additional Expenses

    Owner shall be responsible for all costs directly related to this agreement, including but not limited to transportation, veterinary bills, entries, grooming fees and necessary special equipment. Owner will not be responsible for additional expenses exceeding _____ Dollars ($_____) per month without prior written approval. All additional expenses are due and payable on the first of the month as provided by Section 2.

4. Trainer Responsibilities

    (a) Trainer shall fulfill the duties in a manner consistent with good show training practices in this County of _____ in the State of _____:

    1.

    2.

(b) Trainer shall pay all expenses according to Section 2, sending Owner an accounting each month.

In the event Trainer is not reimbursed on time, Trainer is authorized to deduct said payments from any other source available to Trainer.

(c) Trainer shall obtain all necessary veterinary and farrier services and as agent may authorize direct billing. Any extraordinary care over and beyond normal and regular maintenance requires prior written approval by Owner unless involving the most immediate emergency treatment.

5. Showing

(a) Any Prize money won by Owner's horse while under this agreement shall be treated as follows:

   1.

   2.

(b) Owner's horse(s) shall be shown in name of _____ with _____ as Owner and _____ as Trainer.

6. Lay-ups

If said horse(s) is out of training for over _____ days consecutively, Owner shall pay the cost of board at _____ Dollars ($_____) per day plus incidental expenses as required. Owner must be notified within _____ (_____) days if horse is taken out of training.

7. Term and Termination

(a) The term of this Agreement shall be _____ basis. Either party may terminate Agreement given _____ (_____) days written notice, provided a final accounting by the Trainer is presented and all payments have been made by Owner prior to taking possession of said horse(s).

(b) On termination, Trainer shall have a lien on said horse(s) under _____ law for all unpaid charges on account. Payment must be made in full before said horse(s) is released unless Trainer consents in writing.

8. Insurance

(a) Owner shall bear all risk of loss from the death of or any harm to said horse(s) unless such loss is caused by gross negligence of Trainer, his agents, or employees, in which case Trainer shall bear such loss.

(b) Trainer agrees/does not agree to carry insurance protecting Owner against any losses caused by negligence of Trainer, his agents and employees.

(c) Owner agrees to reimburse Trainer _____% of the premium for said insurance.

(d) Trainer agrees/does not agree to maintain liability insurance.

   1. $_____ per person
   2. $_____ per accident
   3. $_____ property damage

If insurance is so provided, Trainer will make a copy of the policy available to Owner.

9. Indemnification

Owner agrees to indemnify Trainer unless otherwise provided by insurance against all liability or claims, demands, and costs for or arising out of this agreement unless such are caused by the gross negligence of Trainer, his agent or employees.

10. Binding Effect

(a) The parties hereto agree that this Agreement shall be binding on their respective heirs, successors and assigns.

(b) Failure of either party to abide by and perform any and all other terms, covenants, conditions, and obligations of this Agreement shall constitute a default and shall, in addition to any other remedies provided by law or in equity, entitle the wronged party to reasonable attorney fees and court costs related to such breach.

(c) In all respects, this Agreement shall be construed in accordance with, and governed by the laws of _____.

(d) This Agreement contains the final and entire agreement between parties and neither they nor their agents shall be bound by any terms, conditions, or representatives unless amended to this Agreement and initialed by both parties hereto.

IN WITNESS WHEREOF, the parties have executed this Agreement on the day and year first above written.

OWNER: TRAINER:

_____   _____
Signature   Signature

_____   _____
Address   Address

_____   _____

_____   _____
Telephone   Telephone

RELEASE AND HOLD HARMLESS AGREEMENT

The Undersigned assumes the unavoidable risks inherent in all horse-related activities, including but not limited to bodily injury and physical harm to horse, rider, and spectator.

    In consideration, therefore, for the privilege of riding and/or working around horses at _____ _____, located at _____, the Under-signed does hereby agree to hold harmless and indemnify _____ and further release them from any liability or responsibility for accident, damage, injury, or illness to the Undersigned or to any horse owned by the Undersigned or to any family member or spectator accompanying the Undersigned on the premises.

_____

Signature

_____

Print Name, Address, and Telephone Number

_____

_____

_____

Signature of Parent or Guardian

STABLE RECORD

Horse _____   Birth Date _____
Description _____   Height _____
Acquired from _____   Date _____
General Info: _____
_____

	199			
Worming				
Tubed				
Flu Vaccine				
Eastern/Western				
Tetanus				
PHF				
Rabies				
Rhinomune				
Coggins				
Teeth floated				
Other:				

Date	Shoeing	Injury or Sickness/Treatment